CW00522025

Power Through Metaphysics

Volume I

Metaphysical Collection
CONNY MÉNDEZ
(1898-1979)

EDICIONES GILUZ
BIENES LACÓNICA, C. A.
DISTRIBUIDORA GILAVIL, C. A.
2020

Original title in Spanish: *Metafísica 4 en 1*, Volumen I
Méndez, Conny, 1898-1979
Copyright © 1991, 2001, 2020 Distribuidora Gilavil, C.A.

First edition, May 1991
Reprint, September 1996
Reprint, March 1999
Reprint, May 2003
Reprint, April 2004
First edition revised, November 2020

ISBN-10:   980-6114-81-7
ISBN-13: 978-980-6114-81-4

Translated by Bienes Lacónica, C.A., Alexandra Rincones T. and Donald Rincones M.
Edited by Ediciones Giluz
Cover and text layout Diego Gil Velutini
Published and distributed by Distribuidora Gilavil, C.A.
Caracas, Venezuela
Tel: +58 (212) 762 49 85
Tel: +58 (212) 762 39 48
E-mail: infolibros@metafisica.com

www.connymendez.com - www.metafisica.com

Books by Conny Méndez

English, Italian, French and Japanese:

Power Through Metaphysics, Volume I
Power Through Metaphysics, Volume II

Spanish:

Metafísica al alcance de todos
Te regalo lo que se te antoje
El maravilloso número 7
Quién es y quién fue el Conde de Saint Germain
Piensa lo bueno y se te dará
¿Qué es la Metafísica?
El Librito Azul
Un tesoro más para ti
El Nuevo Pensamiento
La Voz del «Yo Soy»
La carrera de un átomo
Numerología
Decretos de Conny Méndez
Pequeño método para comprender la Biblia
Metafísica 4 en 1, Volumen I
Metafísica 4 en 1, Volumen II
Metafísica 4 en 1, Volumen III
El Libro de Oro de Saint Germain (an original translation of *The "I AM" Discourses* by Godfrè Ray King)
Misterios develados (an original translation of *Unveiled Mysteries* by Godfrè Ray King)
La Mágica Presencia (an original translation of *The Magic Presence* by Godfrè Ray King)

Palabras de los Maestros Ascendidos, Volumen I y II (an original translation of *Ascended Master Light* by the Great Cosmic Beings through Godfrè Ray King)

La chispa de Conny Méndez. Humor y memorias (autobiography/humor/caricature)

Cien Años de Amor y Luz (music CD)

Conny Méndez instrumental (music CD)

La Cucarachita Martina (children's music CD and book)

Books by other authors:

Los secretos de Enoch (an original translation by Luisa de Adrianza of *The Enoch Secrets* by Enoch)

El Espíritu de Navidad (Luis Loero y Marcelo Valero)

Los cristales y los signos del mes (Luis Loero y Marcelo Valero)

Available in soft cover, audio books and e-book at
www.connymendez.com

For more information on Conny Méndez, please visit:
Web: www.connymendez.com
YouTube: www.youtube.com/ConnyMendezMetafisica
Facebook: www.facebook.com/ConnyMendezMetafisica
Twitter: @connymendez
Instagram: @connymendez

Power Through Metaphysics

Volume I

Metaphysical Collection
CONNY MÉNDEZ
(1898-1979)

EDICIONES GILUZ
BIENES LACÓNICA, C. A.
DISTRIBUIDORA GILAVIL, C. A.

A Word of Caution to the Reader[1]

The text herein is not considered by the Publishers to contain any detrimental or derogatory and/or religious beliefs or trends present or past. Hence any material contained in this book tending to modify or alter its contents and contravene the editorial policy must be considered as having been included ex post facto, conflicting with the original text which is protected by international copyright law.

Therefore, let it be known that Distribuidora Gilavil, C.A. and Ediciones Giluz (formerly Bienes Lacónica) as Publishers of this edition, copyrighted in 1991 and 2020, in its present format, has not authorized its reprinting by any other party or parties, firms, publishers, organizations, associations, private groups, person, et al. Furthermore, the material contained in this edition may only be distributed through the approved sales outlets of Distribuidora Gilavil, C.A. and/or by written authorization from the Publishers.

No part of his book maybe used or reproduced in any manner whatsoever without written permission by the Publishers, except in the case of brief quotations embodied in critical articles and reviews,

---

1 Translator's note: We ask that today's reader kindly forgive the conventional use of the masculine third-person-singular personal pronoun "he" used throughout the book, as well as the traditional masculine attribution ascribed to God in the Bible (for example, as "Father"). Conny always taught that God possessed no sex or gender.

with its respective reference of the author's full name, book name, date and page number.

The existence of certain unauthorized printings of the Spanish version made this caveat emptor necessary.

THE PUBLISHERS

Preface

*D*uring her lifetime, Conny Méndez would regularly travel to the United States and throughout Latin America, speaking week after week to ever-growing groups of Metaphysical followers eager to hear her thoughts on dynamic Christianity and the ultimate meaning of life. It was not surprising that the mails were heavy with expressions of gratitude from people who felt that she had given significance, purpose and satisfaction to the living of their days. Nor was it surprising that the publication of her books and articles should bring massive response, swelling to worldwide response from the Spanish-reading public.

Over 41 years after Conny Méndez's passing, the response continues. Lives are still being changed by the impact of her books. So it occurred to us that many English-speaking students of Metaphysics could benefit from her writings, excerpts of which had been originally penned into English. (Conny was fluently bilingual having been educated in both the United States and Venezuela).

We undertook to compile and organize all her unpublished English notes relating to the bestselling *Metafísica 4 en 1*. The balance of the material was culled from the published Spanish volumes. Through careful editing, painstaking interpretative translation, and intimate knowledge of her style, our associates and family were able to preserve faithfully the personality and accuracy of Conny's writing.

Here is *Power through Metaphysics,* Volume 1 which we lovingly offer to you who may prefer reading it in English. It too will surely bring prosperity, well-being and new meaning to your life, while helping you to realize your God-given potential.

THE PUBLISHERS

Acknowledgments

*W*e owe deep gratitude to Donald Rincones Méndez, Julieta Velutini Méndez and her son, Diego Gil Velutini, for their unwavering support and inspiration in helping make this book a reality. Our special gratitude goes to Donald's daughter, Alexandra Rincones, who took on a great part of the work, and his dear friends and associates for their invaluable and insightful assistance in the preparation of the English version.

THE PUBLISHERS

Table of Contents

Book II

Your Heart's Desire

Book III

The Mystical Number 7

Book IV

Who is and Who was The Count Saint-Germain

Part I

Part II

Illustrations

Book I

Metaphysics for Everyone

Introduction

*T*his book is not written for academic study; it is written to be understood and used. A college degree in psychology, philosophy or metaphysics isn't required: All you need is a desire to achieve a richer, more fulfilling life and apply the basic truths you'll find in these pages.

It is estimated that we use only about 10% of our brain cells—10% of our potential mental powers. But those dormant, unused cells are there, waiting, ready to be awakened every time we hear or read or experience something new to us. And the second time we come across that new thought or experience, more cells are aroused, more connections are made, and we understand it a little better. Within a short while, the mind becomes "enlightened" as more and more awakened cells begin to work on the new concept. In other words, the acceptance and understanding of ideas is an automatic process that begins with the simple activity of repetition. There is no superhuman effort, no burst of genius required—only the desire to learn and the patience to read and re-read until the ideas behind the words become automatic, and suddenly (or so it seems) understanding is there. It's that simple.

Carry this book with you. Keep a copy next to your favorite chair or the bedside table. Read and re-read—especially when you are faced with a problem or with a distressing life situation. You'll discover something truly amazing: You will open the book at random and within a few sentences, you'll find yourself thinking "This could have been written for me!" And you'll be right. It was.

Jesus Christ said, "In my Father's house, there are many mansions." Metaphysics is one of these "mansions" (or dimensions); it is the study of mental/spiritual laws. (It does not deal with "spiritualism" itself, although this is another of those "mansions.")

This little book has brought peace, fulfillment and prosperity to many. May it bring them to you. And may you be blessed.

CONNY MÉNDEZ

Dynamic Christianity

*B*efore you undertake any job, from a career to tuning up your own car, you have to know something about it. You go to school. You apprentice yourself to someone skilled in that particular enterprise. It is just good sense.

And yet there is one job we all find ourselves thrust blindly into, untrained, uneducated, without the vaguest idea of the hazards involved or the goals to be achieved. And it's the most difficult job on earth.

The job of life.

To make it even more confusing, we don't even know what life is all about. It's full of contradictions. Why do some, born with wealth, health and good fortune turn all these advantages into a downward spiral of misfortune and misery? Why do others achieve good fortune without visible effort? We search for the logic behind these contradictory facts, the rules of the game we find ourselves caught up in: We make guesses, suppositions and we indulge in wishful thinking. And still, most of us are as puzzled at the hour of our death as we were at the hour of our birth. What was it all about?

There is one great Truth that can guide us in the direction of understanding: What you think… is, Thoughts are things. And your thoughts, your attitudes are what will determine everything that happens in your life. What you think about yourself, about others, about the world and events that surround you controls your life. And you are at the controls.

Like all great truths, this fact is startlingly simple to put into words. If you think you are healthy, you will be healthy. But if you turn your thinking around, and begin to fear illness, you will feel ill. And feeling sick is being sick. If you were born to riches, it's likely that you will continue to grow in wealth—unless someone convinces you that "destiny" exists, and that you have no control over it; then any little setback will magnify itself into a catastrophe. You will begin to believe that your fortunes have changed—and once you believe that, they will change. Your life and everything that happens to you is a product of the beliefs you hold and the words you say. This is a principle, a basic, unchanging law called The Principle of Mentalism.

If you believe that accidents lurk around every corner just waiting to happen to you, if you are convinced that the ailments of old age are inevitable, if you are certain that bad luck dogs your very step, all these beliefs will manifest themselves in everything you do. But just the opposite is equally true: If you believe that only good will come to you, then it will. This is called a self-fulfilling prophecy. When you make a prediction, good or bad, you begin to make it come true.

We are never conscious of all the ideas that inhabit our minds. Their formation is continuous, building on everything we hear, see and learn. Yet our actions are the product of those ideas—the majority of which lie below the level of conscious thought. We are just as ignorant of the very laws that govern our lives, the so-called "laws of creation" and we spend our lives haphazardly constructing conditions which conflict with those laws. Blindly, with neither compass nor rudder, we go on watching grand ideas turn into disappointments, blaming our failures on life itself—and chalking it all up to "the will of God."

Since you've read this far, you've probably begun to realize that a human being is not, as you may have been led to believe, a sea-tossed cork with no direction other than the whims of the elements. Far from it! Man's life, his world, his circumstances and the events of his life are the products of his creation, and his alone. He is the ruler of his own mental empire—and if he chooses to believe that he is that storm-wracked cork, he's free to be so.

Free is the key word here. To be born with free will means to have that individual right to choose one's own direction. We can think positively or negatively, optimistically or pessimistically. We can think of evil and ugliness and bring them into being. Or we can think of beauty, goodness and happiness—and create them for our environment, external and internal.

Metaphysics has always taught that what we think about most strongly, most often passes into our subconscious, where it establishes itself and becomes a reflex. Modern psychology has recently "discovered" this ancient truth.

When a human being finds himself immersed in the ocean of his ignorance—in a disaster of his own making—he will usually turn to God and pray for deliverance from this misery. And it appears that sometimes God will hear, and sometimes not. If not, family and friends will offer the inadequate consolation that it is "God's will." It sounds like another way of saying God's ill will, at least to the person involved. But this is in direct conflict with what we have been taught about the Creator. He is our Father, full of love and compassion, infinitely wise, eternally and mercifully with us. How can such a wise and loving father allow such suffering to His own children? We, as merely mortal parents, could never bring ourselves to inflict such punishment on our children. We could not condemn a child to eternal flames for making the natural mistakes of childlike ignorance. Yet we seem to believe that God could do so, that he has all the characteristics of a capricious schoolmaster, one who is petulant, vindictive and full of ill will, always on the watch for the slightest misdeed and quick to subject us to the most unfair and disproportionate punishments.

This is the way we thought in our infancy, before we learned the rules of behavior. And this is the way we must continue to think—until we learn the rules of life.

We have already learned that the calamities of life are of our own creation. And this is one way in which we are fashioned in God's "image and likeness"; we are, each and every one of us, the creators of our own circumstances.

Why is it then, that God seems to hear us at some times and not at others? The answer lies in the nature of prayer. Prayer is the purest and highest form of thought; it is polarizing the mind to the highest possible degree. When we pray, when we think of and toward God, we create vibrations of mental light, and thoughts of God transform the darkness surrounding us, as if we brought a brilliant lamp into the darkest of rooms. And if we pray to God as a loving, caring Father who wishes nothing but joy and fulfillment to His children, He will listen.

But if we pray, as so many of us do, in terms such as: "Please, God, solve this problem for me, even though I know I somehow deserve to be miserable and this is all some kind of test of my worth which I don't understand…" well, all we are telling him is that we really don't think our prayers are worthy of being answered.

Furthermore, we are praying to that malevolent schoolmaster, that vindictive God who likes nothing better than to condemn us for our transgressions. In other words, we're praying to the wrong God! And, to paraphrase, you get what you pray for.

God is not the judge, the policeman, the tyrant or the executioner that so many of us have been taught. He is simply The One who created the laws of existence. Whether we choose to abide by them or ignore them is our decision—and the results of such a decision are our doing. There are seven of these laws, Seven Principles that govern all things at all times. They are unchanging and unending: They are the order and harmony of all creation.

The soul has no need for policemen or judges, for he who does not abide by these laws creates his own punishment. Therefore, once you have learned these laws, and have learned to think correctly, you will automatically be following the laws, and all the good that God wishes for you will show itself!

Saint Paul said that God is closer to us than our feet, our hands, the very air we take into our lungs. We do not have to shout for Him to hear. Merely thinking of Him is enough; the disarray of our lives will begin to rearrange itself into order. He created us and knows us better than we can know ourselves. He knows why we behave as we do, and He does not expect us to behave as saints when we are only learning to walk in this spiritual life.

At this point, I don't want you to believe a single word I have written without proving it to yourself. This is your divine and sovereign right. Don't do as you have done in the past—accepting all you are told and all that you see at face value—until you have taken the opportunity to judge for yourself between good and evil.

The Mechanics of Thought

*A*wake or asleep, we spend 24 hours a day in unceasing thought. Like an unedited film, disconnected thoughts run through our minds, triggered by every sight, sound, smell, taste, touch or experience. And a few of these thoughts we hold and examine more closely than the rest. Why? Because these few have stimulated some feeling within, whether a feeling of fear or repulsion, affection or attraction. It isn't the nature of the feeling, but the strength of it, the interest it holds; and so we concentrate on it, perhaps mention it to someone else. It is this repetition, this strength of interest that leads a thought into the unconscious where it is engraved in memory. This is the process of meditation.

Once an idea is etched into the subconscious, it becomes a "reflex." Just as your leg jerks when the doctor taps you just under the kneecap with his rubber hammer, you experience a feeling, an attitude, a reaction when one of those deeply engraved ideas is touched upon by some event or experience in your life. Your attitude reflects the original feeling you experienced when you first pondered that idea. In metaphysics, we call this a "concept," in the sense of a belief or conviction.

The subconscious is incapable of discrimination. It does not think for itself. It cannot protest, nor does it have free will. Its only function is to summon up a reflex according to a command from the sensory and emotional centers of the conscious mind. In this sense, it is a computer memory, even more complex than the most capacious data storage systems ever made. And it is just as emotionless as a computer; it has no sense of humor, and makes no distinction between an order given jokingly or a serious command. If your nose is a bit larger than the standards of beauty call for, you may jokingly refer to it as a "potato nose" as a minor defense mechanism. But the humorless subconscious will attempt to carry out your "command" in its most literal sense, to make your nose look more and more like your description. And soon it will, to you, because of repetition. So you will unconsciously begin to hold your head a certain way, and repeat that certain phrase so often that others will begin to notice what had probably escaped their attention in the beginning.

The word metaphysics means "beyond the physical." And metaphysics is the science which deals with all things undetectable by the physical senses. It gives reason to things we don't understand, the mysteries that surround us, and all those things that seem not to have a reasonable explanation. Yet, as shrouded as the subject matter may be, metaphysics is a most precise science—a fact you will discover for yourself as you read on.

Do you remember the first time you heard the phrase "catch a cold"? Probably you were too young to remember, but your subconscious does. It was said by your elders, who taught you that a cold was something to be feared, or at least avoided, and with repetition, you adopted their feelings: Never get your feet wet; don't get caught in a draft; stay away from people who are coughing, sneezing or sniffling because you'll soon be doing the same. Little by little, this became engraved on your subconscious, forming a reflex center. You never had to think about it to heed these warnings; the reflex did it for you. And the damage was done, because your subconscious will do its best to give you all the symptoms of a cold whenever you get caught in one of those "cold-catching" situations. Some people don't even need the situations. Once they hear about a "bug that's going around," a tickle begins in the back of their throats.

We know today that wet feet or open windows don't cause colds, but the idea is already there, firmly implanted and rooted to resist the firm tugs of reason. And radio and TV have done their best to nourish those erroneous roots.

All the influences of your formative years have become reflexes such as this—and these are the automatic causes of all that is bad, all that is good that happens to you. These reflexes are your life pattern, a basement full of other people's ideas, which affect every facet of your life, body, soul and mind. But the important point is that, if you had not accepted these ideas, if they hadn't been pounded into you like a nail into wood, if you have been able to exercise your free will, no germ or virus, no power on earth could have been able to make your subconscious react in any other way than the way you wished.

Your will, negative or positive, is the magnet that attracts those germs or viruses in your direction, with a force far stronger than the actual circumstances of a germ-laden environment.

Again, I stress: Your negative or positive attitude towards the facts is what will determine the outcome for you.

The Infallible Formula

*W*e have found that the human mind is a storehouse of accumulated opinions, concepts and convictions, many of which are contrary to truth and in conflict with the basic Principles of Creation. It is these erroneous thoughts which manifest themselves as the sufferings and problems that afflict us: sickness, accidents, pain, arguments, disharmony, poverty, failure and even death.

None of these misconceptions fits within the boundaries of Truth. And, fortunately, there are ways to erase these false beliefs and replace them with truths, which will not only produce the happy and positive conditions we desire, but will prevent the return of those negative influences. With the establishment of Truth in our subconscious minds, the order has been changed; the magnet has reversed its polarity and it becomes impossible to attract the negative factors which no longer produce any response from us.

The infallible formula is simply this: Whenever something undesirable happens to you—you fall ill, have an accident, are robbed, are offended or emotionally hurt by someone; you have been the cause of hurt to another; you have been afflicted by a physical, moral or character defect; you find yourself hating another; you suffer from the pangs of too much love or jealousy or love misdirected; you are the victim of injustice—if any from the infinite list of misfortunes that can befall a human being happens to you... you must seek and know the truth.

Jesus Christ, the greatest of the Metaphysical Masters, said, "Ye shall know the truth, and the truth shall make you free." (John

8:32) What is the Truth? Simply, it is perfect harmony. And if what is happening to you is not born of harmony, justice, goodness, freedom, health, wisdom, love, joy… then it is not Truth. It acts in contradiction to the supreme harmony. It is a lie.

Your higher self is a perfect being, It always has been. It cannot become ill because it is life. Because it is life, it cannot die. It cannot age, suffer, fear nor sin. It has no need to fight. It is unchanging. It is beautiful. It is love, intelligence, wisdom and joy. In this, you have the Truth—your Truth and mine, the Truth of every human being at this moment and for all time.

That isn't to say that every human being is God. No more than a single drop of water is the ocean. But that drop is a part of the ocean, and contains within itself all that is the ocean. From a molecule's viewpoint, that droplet is oceanic in dimension.

It has been stated that whatever you project, whatever is happening to you, whatever you are doing or suffering that goes against Perfect Harmony is due to an erroneous belief within you which is manifesting itself outside you because of your own reflex. This has nothing to do with your essence, your superior being. This is unchangeable, and its conditions and circumstances are at all times perfect.

And so, when faced by adverse circumstances such as those mentioned a few paragraphs ago, keep in mind what I have said and apply the Truth, simply by saying, mentally or out loud: "I do not accept it."

Say it firmly but with infinite gentleness. Mental efforts do not need physical force; neither thought nor soul have, or require, muscles; their strength derives from spiritual forces. So, when you say, "I do not accept it," do so as though you were saying, "I don't want this." Calmly, yet with complete conviction and firmness, without shouting, violence or display. You are making a statement.

After having made your statement, remember that your higher self, that superior being, together with all its conditions, is perfect. NOW say, "I declare the Truth of this problem to be (harmony, love, intelligence, justice, abundance, life, health—any and all positive qualities which oppose the negative condition in which you find yourself). Thank you, Father, for I know you have heard me."

At this point, there is no need for you to believe what you are reading. You must only believe what you say. That you do not, will not accept this situation. That it is contrary to harmony. That harmony will be restored. If you believe and apply these thoughts, you will soon come to believe in their power.

In the language of metaphysics, this is called a "treatment," and for it to be effective, a positive attitude must be maintained. This continuing positive reinforcement is what builds a new reflex, to replace the negative one which brought about unwanted circumstances. Belief begins with hope, not with doubt. Therefore, you cannot doubt the efficacy of the treatment, nor can you express the previous concepts, opinions and beliefs which led to the unpleasant situation; such words would only nullify the positive effect.

St. Paul said "But be ye transformed by the renewing of your mind." (Romans 12:2) This is the purpose of the treatment: Transforming the mental pattern that has been dominating the subconscious, the mental climate that has created the negative environment in which you have been living. This total "transformation" comes with the changing of each old, inharmonious belief as it arises in life (or in the conscience)—changing, "renewing" such beliefs to conform to the Truth.

Metaphysically expressed, those convictions which have become most deeply embedded are called "Crystallizations." While these require much more effort to erase than others, each and every denial or disharmony and affirmation of Truth erodes away at the false concepts until we are left with nothing but the Truth.

And with the establishment of Truth, you will discover miracles in every aspect of your life.

What you see as defects within yourself are only illusions; once you know the Truth—the perfection of the higher self—the illusion of these flaws will fade and disappear. And you will be made again in your perfect form, the true self, your personal Christ, the image of the Father in which you were made. Any student of Christian Metaphysics will confirm this. Never forget this great Truth. Practice it from this moment on. The longer you act upon it, the greater the results you will see in your personal evolution toward perfect harmony.

Remember that you are as unique as your fingerprints. You are one of a kind, created to fulfill a purpose no one else can achieve. It has taken many thousands of years of evolution to produce the you that exists today. God's works are infinite, and you and I are but two expressions of His creation. You must remember, too, that your Christ is wisdom itself; he is God's highest expression of love for itself; He is God's highest expression of love for humankind and He has been waiting these many centuries for you to recognize Him. Now the moment of recognition has arrived. Talk to Him; consult Him; wait for His answer. Once you have come to understand and accept that He is your supreme guide and teacher, you will witness his rebirth. Christ is the Messiah, and his coming is prophesied for this era. This isn't to say that he will dwell among us in the flesh, but that we can all find him born once again in our hearts and minds, which are his kingdom. This is why He was called Christ, the Greek word for Messiah, or "anointed king" in Hebrew.

The Decree

*E*very spoken word is a decree which is outwardly manifested. The word is a spoken thought—and we have already learned of the power of thought.

There are two sayings of Jesus that have not been studied closely enough. One of these is: "For by thy words thou shalt be justified, and by thy words thou shalt be condemned." Most have interpreted this as meaning that others will judge us by what we say and write, and though this is true, it is not the full meaning of Christ's own words. Jesus taught the truths of metaphysics at a time when the majority of the human race was not sufficiently mature to understand it. He was aware of this, and a number of times He said that there was much that he had to say, but that we would not be able to understand. But there would always be a few who understood and would instruct others: "Who hath ears, let him hear." The second reference he made to the power of words was this: "Not that which goeth into the mouth defileth a man, but that which cometh out of the mouth, this defileth a man, for out of the abundance of the heart the mouth speaketh." In this response to a trivial question about dietary law lies a great metaphysical truth in all its explicit beauty.

I suggest that you spend a day just listening to yourself—to the "decrees" you make so casually: "Business is rotten." "Kids today are a lost generation." "We'll never get there in this traffic." "You can't trust anyone these days." "It's not safe to walk the streets." "Don't touch that; you'll break it." "With my luck, I'll probably (fill in your favorite disaster)." "I've never seen it to fail." "I love _____, but it upsets my stomach." "I can feel one of those migraines coming on."

"He'll rob you blind." "She's a vicious gossip." "There's no point in trying."

You can see the pattern. You've made the prophecies, and your attitudes govern your actions to the point where you make sure those prophesies are fulfilled. Never forget: Every word you utter is a decree, whether positive or negative. When it is positive, it is manifested in good; when negative, only bad can follow. If your words are against someone, it's the same as condemning yourself; that person lives up (or down) to your expectations—at least where you are concerned. But when you speak with kindness and understanding toward others, they will return kindness and understanding to you. And when something unpleasant happens to you, don't think, "I wasn't expecting that!" Think instead of statements you have made in the past that predicted— and literally caused—your misfortune. It could have been one of those idle statements, like those above. ("Every time I make an investment, I lose my shirt.")

Jesus was not one to waste words, and he expressed himself eloquently in saying: "For out of the abundance of the heart the mouth speaketh." He is telling us that it is the feeling that accompanies a thought which engraves it upon the subconscious and gives it its power. The first feeling we learn is fear, taught to us by our parents in their desire to keep us from harm, by religious teachers in their desire to keep us from wrongdoing. Fear makes our hearts accelerate; we say, "My heart jumped into my throat," when we speak of great fear we've felt. And it is that fear "from the heart" that lies behind all the negative phrases mentioned above.

St. Paul said that we would be transformed by the renewing of our minds. But how is this renewal accomplished? Start with your negative statements; each time you find yourself saying something negative, you've pulled out an erroneous concept that was buried in your subconscious, and you'll recognize the feeling that goes along with it. Erase it. Whether the emotion is fear, dislike, despair or anger, deny it as a lie and then affirm the Truth, so that it will no longer manifest itself in your actions. You'll soon find that you speak differently, and your way of thinking has changed with this practice. Both you and your life will be transformed by this renewal of your mind.

Increase your awareness of others. In the company of others, observe their language, and the actions which bear out their statements; you'll be aware of their concepts by the results they bring upon themselves. Do not agree with what you hear when conversations turn negative. Think instead: "I do not accept it, for myself or for them." You don't have to tell them about the truth you are learning; in fact, it's best not to, not because it is some secret ritual, but because they may not yet be ready for it. There is a proverb: "When the student is ready, the teacher appears." People who are ready for advancement are automatically drawn to those who can lead them; it's a basic law of attraction, so there is no need for you to be a "Missionary." Trying to force the truth on people usually drives them in the other direction. This is what Jesus referred to when He said: "Give not that which is holy to dogs, neither cast ye pearls before swine, lest they trample them under their feet and turn against you and rend you."

Faith can Move Mountains

*Y*ou have heard this proverb repeated again and again. But it is usually said thoughtlessly, since few people really know what it means, nor why or how faith can "move mountains."

Fear, too, can move mountains—for fear is merely a negative form of faith: Faith in evil. It is the firm conviction that something bad is going to happen. Pure faith, on the other hand, is the certainly that whatever happens will be good.

You don't fear that something good will happen to you. Nor do you say, "I have faith that something bad is coming." Faith is what we wish for. And you don't wish for harm to come to you: you fear it!

But you attract what you fear—and so it comes about. And when it does happen, you may say—with a kind of perverse triumph—"I knew it! I could feel it!" And so you did—but don't go around boasting of your clairvoyant skills. What happened was that you thought about this or that misfortune with fear. You did indeed predict it, with words and with emotions. And you have learned once again that whatever you think about with strong emotional intensity will come to pass. You fully expected it. And to expect, to anticipate, is to have faith, negative or positive.

So, now that you know that everything you anticipate with faith will come to you—what's to stop you from using that knowledge, that faith, to answer your every wish? It is a natural law, a divine ordinance. Christ said so in these familiar words: "And all things whatsoever ye shall ask in prayer, believing, ye shall receive." (Mark 21:22) St.

Mark, too, stated specifically: "Whatsoever things you desire, when ye pray, believe that ye receive them, and ye shall have them." Saint Paul expressed it more broadly: "Faith is the substance of things hoped for, the evidence of things not seen." We have defined faith as the conviction of good. That conviction doesn't come out of thin air—it comes from knowledge, and that knowledge from experience. When you take a trip to a distant city, whether by air, train or car, you're rarely afraid of missing a turn and ending up on the moon. Perhaps a stone-age man, without benefit of the knowledge of maps or airline schedules would be shaking with fear at the prospect, but you, with the knowledge of a civilized world at your disposal, know where you are going and when you are scheduled to arrive. This is faith, based on awareness, or knowledge.

People fear evil, and do not know to apply faith—or even have the slightest notion of what faith is—because they lack knowledge of the Principles of Creation.

Faith is conviction, certainty. But these must be based on specific knowledge. You know that a certain distant city exists. That people often go there, that you can get there—and that the moon is nowhere near your destination.

This is positive faith. The converse is equally true: If you want something and fear that you won't get it—you won't. Simply because you denied yourself what you wanted in advance. Very likely, your prayer was designed more to prepare yourself for disappointment than for fulfillment: "Oh, Lord, grant me this, even though I know I don't deserve it and I'll understand if you don't because You probably don't think it's right for me." That's negative prayer. And it works. Negatively.

Now let's try the positive. There's a metaphysical formula for getting anything you want. Use it for everything. Don't believe it simply because I say it. Try it; let it work for you. (Your faith, your belief must come with your own experience, your own knowledge!) Your positive prayer: "I wish for this. I wish it to be in harmony with the universe and according to God's will, His grace and His perfection. I thank you Father, for I know You have heard me."

You must not doubt for an instant. You have used a formula that some would call magic—which metaphysicians know is an application of universal principles. If you have fulfilled the law with complete belief you will get your wish. But be patient. The more calmly you await fulfillment, the sooner you shall see results. Impatience, tension and mental stress destroy the treatment (as it is called in metaphysics).

Let me explain the importance of the wording in this formula. By saying, "In harmony with the universe," you avoid the danger of bringing harm to another in fulfilling your wish, and make it impossible for you to wish harm to another. By saying, "According to God's will," you acknowledge that God may see that what you specifically want may be less than perfect, or even harmful, for you; in which case He will substitute something even better than you had hoped for. In other words, you are asking God to make your wish as good as your intentions.

The words, "His grace and His perfection" contain the ultimate safeguards. Let me give you an example of what can happen if you do not seek God's grace and perfection. A lady was hard-pressed for a specific amount of money, and she asked for it in specific terms, for the 15th of the month. She firmly believed that she would be granted her wish—but her selfishness and indifference did not inspire her to ask in a way that would consider the welfare of others. The next day, her daughter was hit by a car and, precisely on the 15th of that month, she received the exact amount asked for—in the form of an insurance settlement for her daughter's accident. She used the formula incompletely, and thus worked against the law, against even her own self interest.

To ask for something in God's grace and perfection is to work with the spiritual law. The law of God is always on that perfect, spiritual level, where there are no obstacles or setbacks, no harm befalls anyone, no fights or struggles can take place. Here, all things run smoothly, tempered with great love. This is that great Truth you are beginning to know—that will make you free.

"I thank you Father, for I know you have heard me" is the ultimate expression of faith which we can pronounce. Jesus taught and applied that faith when He broke the bread that fed five thousand people, or changed water into wine at the wedding feast. We celebrate that faith by saying grace before a meal. We thank God for his graciousness before we experience its manifestation.

As you read on, you will begin to see that everything Christ taught was metaphysical.

Everything you wish for or need is waiting for you, waiting to manifest itself in response to your wish or prayer. God has already provided everything, and we have only to ask for these blessings as the need arises. All we have to remember is that we must never ask that any harm befall another person, because that harm, or its backlash, will fall upon us. And whatever we ask for ourselves must be asked for all mankind, in the name of harmony, for we are all children of the same Father.

And He is a generous Father. Therefore, pray for abundance. Don't say, "Oh, Lord, please give me a place to live, just a small apartment, that's all I ask," when your large family needs a large house. God's resources are as boundless as His generosity. If you ask for little, little is all you'll receive. Ask instead: "Oh, Lord, give me and all mankind the wonders of your kingdom." And make a list.

The spiritual "muscle" of faith needs as much exercise as your arms and legs. Practice. Make that list of things you want. Make another list of things your life would be better without, from flaws in your character to adverse circumstances that surround you. Read the list every night, with the formula above, feeling no doubt, and give thanks each time you think about or speak aloud your wishes. As your wishes come true, cross them off your list. And, once they have all been granted, don't be so ungrateful as to think that they'd probably have come true anyway. It's simply not true. They were granted because you asked for them in the right way, in good faith, and external aspects were adjusted so that they could happen in a natural way.

Just as we strengthen our positive faith, we must work to weaken that negative faith, the faith in evil which is fear. Sadly, we are all accustomed to fear, for a wide variety of reasons. But the following formula, repeated daily or more often, will wear away that reflex you have embedded in your subconscious: "I AM not afraid. I will not fear. I have faith that God is love and that there is nothing to fear in all of His creation. I will feel only that faith."

When Roosevelt said, "The only thing we have to fear is fear itself," he was voicing a great truth. A truth which you should say to yourself, even when you are shaking with fear—especially then! Once you realize that fear is the great enemy, and not the conditions which make you feel it, you have begun to triumph over that fear. Your verbal wish to dissolve fear and replace it with faith is enough to place you on the positive pole of faith.

You've probably heard about the psychological principle that says the most effective way to break a bad habit is to replace it with a good one. It is a metaphysical principle as well: Once you have begun the treatment of wearing away a deeply implanted reflex, you must fill that blank space with a new and opposite idea. Otherwise that empty space will attract reflexes of the same kind that filled it before—for those reflexes are floating around everywhere, in conversation, in the attitudes of others, looking for fertile ground.

Replacing fear with faith denies those negative thought spaces in the subconscious. The constant repetition of your formula is necessary; remember, it took years for those negative ideas to form, so you must be willing to spend a few minutes a day erasing them. And gradually, you will see things begin to happen just as you positively expect them to happen. Jesus said, "By their fruits, ye shall know them." One meaning of this is that positive events are reflections of a positive faith.

This powerful tool—the power to decree—is an ancient one, first mentioned in the first two Chapters of Genesis. I suggest you take a little time to read them now. As you read, you'll realize that man was not created to be a pawn in a game of circumstances, a victim of situations or some puppet dancing on strings held by powers beyond his control. Quite the opposite: Man was placed at the zenith of creation; rather than being, as some suppose, one of the least significant beings in creation, man was given God's highest authority over earth and its creatures, and the wisdom, if he will use it, to rule his planet in perfection. We are created in God's image, and have been given his powers, including the power of decree. And we have been given free will—the freedom to choose between the perfection that comes with perfect faith and the disharmony that is fear. Man is the means by which the wisdom, love and power of the Creator can be fully expressed.

We have been placed, with all our concerns, in a universe which is obedient to God's will, and has no other alternative than to carry out the decrees of His supreme authority. Still, the authority God has given us is total, and our power to decree is absolute. And, though the basic nature of the universe is perfect in the Creator's eyes, it will appear to man only as man decrees it. The story of the Garden of Eden tells us that man lived in a universe of perfect order, maintaining his powers to think and decree in absolute harmony— until he ate from the tree of knowledge of good and evil. From that point on, the concept that there was an opposite to perfection, and that evil could happen, has plagued mankind. His choices, what he could decree for himself, now included unhappiness in its countless forms. His power had become potentially self-defeating. But it is still within our power to restore the harmony of our own lives, to re-create our own Eden.

Love

*T*his chapter will complete your introduction to the First Principle of Creation. This is the Principle of Mentalism, and it can be summed up as "The Mind is all."

Jesus said, "Ye are Gods." (John 10:34) He meant that the creative capacity of God is within every one of us. Thus, with our thoughts alone, we can create, or re-create, all that we see in our environment, just as the whole of creation was brought into being by a thought. You have already been introduced to the mechanics of this mental creation, the negative or positive character of that which has been created, the force required to determine its nature, the way to change the external aspects of that which you have created by denial or affirmation, the power of the spoken thought as a confirmation of attitude, and finally, the infallible formula for creating and establishing the best possible personal universe for yourself. You are capable of bringing about harmony in your life by following Jesus' advice to "know the truth." And you have discovered that the Truth is that the universe was created in perfection by a perfect being, and that evil has no power when confronted with this truth, because evil is not God's creation, and it must disappear when the truth of faith in perfection is substituted for the thoughts that brought it about. Jesus admonished us, "Resist not evil" not because evil is so powerful, but because it is powerless in the face of Truth—the good, which is the natural state of things.

From now on, you won't have to cast about for someone to blame for your troubles. You merely have to look within and ask, "What was my mental attitude about this situation? Was it positive or negative? Did I have faith or was I afraid? What kind of decrees did I make with my words?" "By their fruits, ye shall know them." Simply be honest with yourself and you will see how you controlled things. If you like what you see, fine. If not, you have within you the power to change your circumstances.

In Christian Metaphysics, we believe God to be seven aspects: Love, Truth, Life, Intelligence, Soul, Spirit and Principle. These are all abstract concepts; we cannot see, feel or hear them, but we can feel and recognize their effects. They exist, act and produce results, and not one of them can be denied. Love is the first aspect of God, the most powerful facet of His "character," and it is the strongest and most sensitive of all forces. But very few of us know what love really is. Most of us think of it as being what we feel for parents, children, spouses, lovers, and so forth. Affection, tenderness, sexual attraction, dislike and hate are all different degrees of sensation—and these sensations only skirt the border of Love in its purest sense. Let us try to focus in on the heart of it by examining the sensations we are familiar with. On this scale, the central, or neutral points are what we call tolerance and goodwill, with love at one extreme and hate and loathing at the other.

This may seem to be unbalanced, since we consider goodwill a positive or loving kind of feeling, but if you think about it, you will see that tolerance and goodwill disappear when we love too much, for these feelings must apply to all, not simply to the object of our exaggerated affections. And, of course, there is no tolerance or goodwill to be found in hatred, for this is the antithesis of love and the absence of goodwill. Jesus said, "peace be unto those of goodwill," which implies that peace is goodwill, and that the extremes are departure, from peace. Peace is at the center; it is the fulcrum of that perfect balance. All excesses unbalance that scale away from this center, away from peace. Even the excess of good things—money, love, prayer, charity, sacrifice, etc. This is what is meant by the "Tree of the knowledge of good and evil" in Genesis: The forbidden fruit is not so much knowledge as it is excess. God Himself only mentions the terms bad or evil in reference to excess. (And in this connection, now would be a good time to pause and read the chapter in Ecclesiastes which begins, "There is a time for everything.")

Too much love? How can that be? But you already know the answer if you've ever seen a mother "love" her children so much that she never allows them to leave their nests, get married or live any kind of independent life. This is not love but a selfish desire to possess. The same is true of jealousy. These are not aspects of love but aspects of excess, and an unbalancing of scale—for there is little peace in such relationship, no room for tolerance and goodwill. Shakespeare understood: Speaking of music as the food of love, he said, "Give me the excess of it, that, surfeiting, the appetite may sicken and so die." Too much love destroys love.

Generally, an excess of feeling is balanced by a corresponding lack of Intelligence—another of the aspects of God. This, of course, will create indignation among people who consider themselves "sensitive." But there is a great difference between sensitivity—which is a form of awareness—and sentimentality, which is allowing one's intelligence to be outweighed by unthinking emotions. Again, it's a matter of balances. If emotion is hot, then intelligence is cold—but peace is neither a polar blizzard nor the blistering heat of the Saharan sun. It is a comfortably warm spring day, a temperate blend of climates. Now, having a great emotional capacity is desirable—if it is balanced by an equal capacity for intelligent thought. This is what makes great artists—their work is the vessel into which they intelligently pour their emotional potential. But the excessively emotive person pours that passion onto those who surround him or her, and the effect is not love but smothering.

If you can recognize this quality in yourself, you have the honesty to correct it. And the method is meditation. Concentrate on the idea of intelligence. Do it daily, for as long as you can. The more time you invest, the better. Begin by asking yourself what intelligence is. Define it in yourself, in humanity. Then go on to consider that everything—plants and animals included—has intelligence. Intelligence, remember, is a sense of awareness, of knowledge. Finalize this by affirming: "I have been created from the essence of God, with, by and from His intelligence; I share the intelligence of God." A few days of this repeated treatment will produce a noticeable increase in your mental elasticity, and in a week you will experience a transformation in the way you feel love for others; there will be a new serenity and generosity which you may never have thought possible. At the same time, you'll notice a change in the way others treat you. We may be all individuals, but what changes one, affects others, all others, in varying degrees. This upward step you take affects all of humanity, starting with those you love most—including yourself.

Now let's deal with humanity's number one enemy—resentment and ill feeling. The generalized feelings which find their culmination in hate. Not one of us is totally free of resentment, yet it can embitter our whole life; it has a bad influence on every event or relationship, and it is the cause of every disappointment we suffer—even though we have learned to "know the truth" and to "deny or affirm" and keep a watch over and correct our thoughts and words. Just one resentment, one ill feeling engraved on the subconscious and the soul is a small fountain of bile, tainting and embittering, going against all of our fondest wishes. Nothing, not even the most perfect situation can endure as long as this emotional pollution exists to poison our every attitude. Religions and holy books are endlessly telling us that we must treat our enemies with forgiveness—for our own sakes, not for theirs! But they do not tell us how. The result is that people play with words: "I can forgive, but I can't forget." But the two are inseparable: If one has not forgotten, one has not truly forgiven, and what memories remain beget resentment.

Fortunately, there is an infallible formula that lets you forgive and forget at the same time, so you can achieve that balance that puts peace and goodwill at the center of your life.

The formula is an effort of love. St. John, often called the "Apostle of Love," repeats the words of the Lord: "If ye keep my commandments, ye shall abide in my love." Love is the fulfillment of the law. It has been said, "The man who loves well is the most powerful man in the world." For that man is of and with God, happy and satisfied with his world.

Again, the formula is simple: Whenever you feel ill will toward someone or feel resentment over something that has been done to you, whenever you recognize open hostility on your part or a desire to take revenge, then you must force yourself to deliberately recall all the good about the person involved—not forgetting what has just occurred to arouse your resentment. Try to relive good times spent in his or her company, the times before resentment set in. Think only of good times, the good qualities about this person. Recall a humorous situation and try to laugh again with the recollection. Once you have achieved this, the miracle has begun. One treatment may not be enough to erase the resentment, but all that's required is repetition, as many times as necessary—and you'll feel the resentment weaken its hold and wash away.

This is the real meaning of "Resist ye not evil," the true way of "turning the other cheek." It is loving one's enemy, blessing those who curse us and praying for those who say evil things about us. By wrapping up bad memories in good ones, we have smothered them into forgettability. Once we have forgotten the feeling of resentment, forgetting the cause of it is automatic! If you do this in all sincerity, you will soon discover a new feeling of freedom. Little things will stop bothering you—and soon, those little annoyances will even stop happening. Your life will begin to run smoothly. Best of all, you will have the goodwill of those around you, even those who may not have liked you before. By creating it within yourself, you have created the same peaceful balance in others.

Denials and Affirmations

Confronting an illness in yourself or another:

I deny the appearance of all physical affliction. I do not accept it for myself or anyone else. The only truth lies within my soul, and all sickness flees like a lie before the Truth of my words. I have faith that life is health, strength and joy and we are all expressions of Life. I thank thee, Father, for I know you have heard me.

Confronting any fear of your own or of another:

I deny fear. Since God did not create fear, it can have no existence except that which I allow it. I reject this appearance which I have created. I let go and banish every shadow of fear within myself or within you. St. John said, "Love dispels all fear." God is love: I am His child, made of and by His love. Thus I dispel fear. I thank thee, Father, for I know you have heard me.

Confronting any sorrow of your own or of another:

I deny the very existence of this sorrow, grief or depression, since it does not come from God. I have no use for negative feelings; I do not accept them; I erase them. God is happiness, pleasure and joy, and, therefore, I AM all of these as well. I thank, thee, Father, for I know you have heard me. And I thank thee for these joys: (list all those good things in your life which bring you joy).

Confronting failure or lack:

I deny the appearance of any lack in my circumstances or myself. I know that only God's abundance is the Truth. I deny failure, for only success and happiness are of God. My world contains everything, and what I desire will come to me, in God's perfection. I know you will show me the way, Lord. I thank thee Father, for I know you have heard me.

Confronting any situation of conflict:

I deny all that which is inharmonious; I do not accept this or any conflict. God is perfect harmony, and there can be no conflict, setback or struggle or any state which opposes the fulfillment of His harmony. I know that the appearance of conflict will vanish. I thank thee, Father, for I know you have heard me.

Confronting all that is in conflict with the peace of the world:

I deny any appearance which is contrary to goodwill, which is the peace of the world. I thank thee for the Truth of thy eternal peace. These events are the creations of those who ignore thy truth, and they are of no importance. Forgive them, for they know not what they do.

Peace is thy will, and thy will be done on earth as it is in heaven. I thank thee, Father, for I know you have heard me.

* * *

I have offered these prayers for you to use as guidelines in creating your own messages or decrees, your own formulas. Remember that we are constantly thinking and expressing attitudes—making decrees—almost every moment of our lives. In other words, we are constantly at prayer. The vital thing to remember is to keep these constant prayers positive. This is the only way to achieve a positive life.

It is important to keep within the spirit of the prayer. The effect of a prayer is destroyed if, after affirming, you let yourself slide back to the negative pole. Be in control of your thoughts and words. Do not let diluting or negating thoughts weaken your prayer. Ignore what others say; remember, they do not know what you are learning.

Never forget that wishing good for one is wishing good for all. What you wish for others will come back to you, and what you wish for yourself, you should also wish for others. Your wishes are more valuable than charitable donations, for these last only for the moment, while Truth remains forever. Wish for all to come to know the Truth. Your wish and the wishes of the millions who have read and will read this book and its companions will enter into the hearts of others, and you will have granted the spiritual gift of knowledge to others. The Principle of Rhythm, like the pendulum or boomerang, returns like to like. "Honni soit qui mal y pense" means "Evil to him who evil thinks." But only good can come to one whose thoughts are good.

It has been said that "God plus one is a majority." This means that one person alone who raises his consciousness to the spiritual plane, using the metaphysical Truth of God, can save an organization from ruin, a community, a city or a nation from crisis. This truth dominates all the planes of existence. "And the Truth shall make you free."

The Metaphysical Meaning of
the Ten Commandments

*T*o this day, it is still unknown whether Moses was who the Bible says he was or was actually the son of the sister of Pharaoh Ramses II. His name—an Egyptian name—means "taken from the waters," and since the Bible is rich in symbolic stories—so written to make sure that the truths these stories are meant to bring us would not be lost in a multitude of translations—the Biblical account of Moses being born a Jew and adopted by the princess could also be more symbolic than historical.

The point is, the truth of his origin has no effect on his teachings. Moses was an enlightened man, a great Master of Metaphysical Truth, who not only freed the Jews from slavery and the subhuman conditions in which they were living, but also spread his teachings to the nomadic bands who joined the tribes of Israel in the desert. This is one reason why the many peoples of the Middle East today are almost entirely monotheistic.

Among these different races, some were more primitive than others. These had no respect for the property of others, who killed those who obstructed them, who allowed the old to die of hunger, since they had outlived their usefulness, and who considered women no more than communal property.

The more civilized Israelites, however, had tasted the lash of slavery and were more inclined to a better treatment of their fellow men, despite the fact that they had fallen in with the idolatrous ways of the Egyptians and varied desert cultures, forgetting the one God of their fathers. This forced Moses to codify their forgotten standards into a simple set of laws that could be understood by all. He decreed harsh punishments for disobedience of these divine laws, believing this the only way to tame the beast within.

Moses had been educated at the Temple at Heliopolis, one of the world's great centers of learning at that time, where he learned Mathematics, Metaphysics, Astrology, Numerology (the meaning of numbers) and a triple symbolism which was used in those days to record knowledge for future generations as they evolved.

This symbology provides insight into Moses' thinking and into the meaning of the Commandments. The first aspect was the simplest, dealing with the everyday life and world of the human being. The second aspect was metaphysical, and dealt with the same conditions as the first, on a more abstract mental level. The last, most profound aspect was hieroglyphical and dealt with human life in a metaphysical sense. (This last aspect was said to be so profound that one, whose soul was absolutely pure, could only understand it.) All aspects were encompassed by the Principle of correspondence, which states: "As it is above, so it is below; as it is below, so it is above." Below and above refer to the physical and spiritual planes, the world of everyday existence and the abstract mental and spiritual world of the soul. What the statement means is simply that all laws act on all levels, and that conditions on one level have their counterparts on the level below and the level above. The importance of these echoes or correspondences will become clearer as we go on.

Moses meant the Ten Commandments (or Sepher Bereshit, as the laws are called in Hebrew) to be understood and obeyed on all levels, so that man would not only be guided but also educated and awakened by them. The interpretations that follow are as old as the Commandments themselves, based on the same symbology Moses learned at Heliopolis and passed on to us by those scholars who have kept this methodology alive through the centuries. And man, for the most part, obeys these laws on the first level. There are many who complain about the contradictions between dogma and common sense, people who accept the rightness of the Commandments but are searching for a higher understanding of things, including the laws we live by. That higher understanding is what this ancient interpretation provides.

Let us sum up the Ten Commandments on their literal level:

1. There is but one God; thou shalt not worship any other.
2. Thou shalt not make or worship false images.
3. Thou shalt not take the name of God in vain.
4. Thou shalt keep the Sabbath day holy.
5. Thou shalt honor thy father and thy mother.
6. Thou shalt not kill.
7. Thou shalt not commit adultery.
8. Thou shalt not steal.
9. Thou shalt not bear false witness.
10. Thou shalt not covet.

These laws are of two kinds. Eight of them as prohibitions, having the words, "Thou shalt not." Only numbers 4 and 5 stand out as recommendations. Taken at the literal level, the eight are apparently rules of behavior, outlawing antisocial acts. And to the less civilized societies of those days, such literal prohibitions were necessary. It was not an easy world. People thought in terms of survival, and gave little thought to behavior that did not contribute to that basic need. One did not kill a member of his family or his tribe because it would be killing one of his protectors, and he would be banished into the desert at the least. But when it came to outsiders, the rules were different. An obnoxious Philistine was fair game, it took this codification to declare that killing any fellow human was against God's law. And civilized behavior had to be taught on a legal/habitual basis. Even in those times of relative primitiveness and ignorance, the average person was rarely moved to break the laws. Then as now, it was the minority who ignored the rules. The great majority find the commandments to be natural extensions of the common-sense "Golden Rule." There is still murder, theft, lying and covetousness in the world, true, but these are the act of the minority, those who do not realize that there is indeed a higher law that punishes those who do not live by the rules that protect the rest of society.

But most of humanity is ready to look at the Commandments we take for granted in a new light, from the vantage point of the second aspect of the three-part symbolism of Moses. The Commandments are clear on the literal or physical level. Let's look at them from a purely mental viewpoint. (The hieroglyphic or spiritual level is beyond our understanding today, and will remain so until we reach that total purity of soul that permits total enlightenment.)

Let's examine Commandments 6, 8, 9 and 10, against killing, stealing, bearing false witness and covetousness. At first glance, these are on the same level as "Thou shalt not walk on the grass," although they carry more stringent penalties. These are actions prohibited by authorities, implying that you may choose to disobey, but you'll regret the decision. But there is a difference, on the mental level. It's the difference between shall and will. Most languages make a distinction between these verbs. "Shall" is simply future tense. "Will" is just that—an act of will. "I shall do it" means "It is going to be done by me." "I will do it" means "I choose to do it." The same is true of "Thou shalt not." It doesn't mean "You must not"—it means, categorically, "This is not going to be done by you."

It has been said that the meaning carried by these commandments is equivalent to saying, "Thou shalt not fly to the moon by flapping thine arms." The thought is laughable, even to those who aren't aware of the laws of physics and biology that make the effort an impossibility. "But," you might say, "That's a statement of fact, not a Commandment!" And in saying this, you'll have come to the heart of the matter.

Because, on the mental level, a Commandment is a statement of fact.

Thou Shalt not Kill

"Thou shalt not kill" means that you cannot kill. The material body has no will of its own. It can't oppose or impose anything. Life lies within the soul, the spirit, and the higher self. And when this life leaves its temporary vehicle of flesh and bones, what remains is, indeed, a lifeless body. The person with the knife, the gun, the pinch of cyanide has not taken a life; he has merely caused it to move to the next plane of existence, as conscious as ever. And instead of having removed someone who is an obstacle or threat from his life—he has created an even greater one. The Law of Rhythm is in operation, and the murderer has brought his own death closer; perhaps it will be an accident, a debilitating disease or death at the hands of another. It has happened so often that clichés cover the situation: "He who lives by the sword, dies by the sword." It is not God who punishes, but the inexorable order of His law. His Principle rules over the universe on every plane, both to repay good and to exact the cost of evil. "Order is the first rule in heaven." And every deed is subject to that order, for every human being, every life is recorded: "Ye are counted, unto the last hair upon thy head."

Now you can see why we say that no harm comes to you from any outside force. No one can hurt you unless there is a "record" of your having done something similar to someone else. No one can ruin your reputation, your business, your happiness, your home or any of your belongings—nor can you do damage to those of another. There is no such thing as an accident; nothing happens by pure chance. The great Laws protect you. The vast majority of people feel incapable of killing or bringing harm to another human being. It is against the Commandments; it is against society's laws; it is against the moral "grain" of most individuals. This is our first line of defense. The second line is the second aspect of the Commandments, which tells us that it is impossible to truly accomplish these wrongs, and that our attempts will only bring back the same evil upon us. The boomerang returns to the hurler.

"Thou shalt not kill" is not a limited admonishment, referring only to human beings—any more than it refers to only one tribe or group of human beings. No life is to be dismissed as insignificant. Yet there are times when an animal must be killed for the greater good that will result. Even if we adopt the karmic philosophy and accept the possibility that every living creature, down to the microscopic level, has a spirit capable of evolving through incarnation into the most superior of men, we must adopt a common sense attitude. Common sense is one way by which divine wisdom manifests itself in a human being. This is a fact well worth repeating and memorizing. Say it to yourself whenever you are faced with a doubtful situation.

When thinking of life as the precious thing it is, it becomes impossible to draw a line. Is the kitten or puppy, virtually adopted as a member of the family, more deserving of life than the verminous, disease-bearing rat? Both are highly intelligent animals, equals on the evolutionary scale. What about the venomous serpent, the loathsome cockroach, the infection-producing staphylococcus? All are Life. The same is true of the vegetable kingdom, from the flowers we casually sever from their roots to decorate our homes, to the mold that decorates a forgotten crust of bread—these reproduce their kind, grow and respond to stimuli (even music). These are Life.

In giving us freedom of choice, God has made us judges over his "lesser" creatures. And we have made judgments. Society has laws against the indiscriminate killing of domesticated animals and endangered species. At the same time, society licenses exterminators and stockyard slaughterhouses. We domesticate bees and fumigate wasps. We cultivate the yeasts that produce fine wines and slaughter disease-producing bacteria by the billions.

Common sense has given rise to these laws, and common sense is what we must use on the individual level as well. Let's take a seemingly absurd example. A cockroach scuttles across the floor of your spotless kitchen. Your first instinct is to crush it under your heel, or reach for the Raid. You know that where you see one, there are dozens, perhaps hundreds more. They are a threat to health and cleanliness, and the thought of one crawling on your arm makes your skin do the crawling. Yet the cockroach is one of the most ancient forms of life on earth today, having arrived millions upon millions of years before man, even before the dinosaurs. If longevity is the only guideline, they have more right to be here than we do.

But intelligence outweighs longevity. However, intelligence carries with it responsibility. The words of Genesis 1:26 give us the clue: "Let us make man in our own image, after our likeness. Let him have dominion over the fish of the sea, the birds of the air and the beasts of the field, and over all wild beasts and over the creatures that crawl upon the ground. And thus God created man in His image, in the divine image created He him." (Note that the reference to God's image is repeated three times. This triple repetition appears often in the Bible, and its intention is to emphasize that a statement is valid on the physical, mental and spiritual levels. In other words, no further metaphysical explanation should be sought: The truth is before you, eternal and unchanging.)

"Dominion" is the power of judgment. Even the cockroach should be accorded conscious judgment. Millions of people believe that even the lowest creatures have souls, or are a part of a greater "group soul," and the hive behavior of ants and bees seems to lend evidence to the possibility—heir activities certainly seem to be governed by a well-ordered group consciousness. Compare the activities of ants building a nest—the various groups going about their appointed functions with no apparent communications—with the same activities as at a modern construction site. If contracts were awarded on dogged efficiency alone, we'd have ants building our condominiums. We might compare the functions of the various ant groups to those of various parts of the body—hands, eyes, feet, ears and so forth, all governed by the brain, sent through lines of communication called nerves. Perhaps there is a single intelligence guiding them all.

And perhaps that intelligence occupies an equally significant place in the universe as your own; perhaps it will, in future incarnations, achieve singular intelligence. Hundreds of millions of people believe just that, and I do not consider myself wise enough to scoff at them.

Your approach to the cockroach? Try this: Think strongly, or even say aloud, "There is one cell of this intelligence that is creating disharmony in my environment. I ask the intelligence to remove it and restore harmony."

A surprising number of people who have tried this have said that the roach (spider, lizard or whatever) has literally stopped in its tracks and then changed direction to disappear, never to return. As always, belief in the Truth of harmony must underlie your words. If the creature appears a second time, or others appear, repeat your words, adding, "Take this cell away or I may be forced to kill it." If this does not work, for any number of reasons (perhaps the creature actually seeks its own death as translation to a higher order), then you must kill it swiftly, painlessly and with no emotion other than goodwill: "May you evolve into a higher species." Your well-meaning thought and intention protect you from the consequences of your action.

Many religious groups forbid their followers to eat meat, believing that the vibrations of agony from the animal being killed contaminate the human soul and degrade his physical being as well. Jesus did not agree, saying: "Not that which goeth into the mouth defileth a man, but that which cometh out of the mouth, this defileth a man; for out of the abundance of the heart, the mouth speaketh." And Moses said, "Not anyone nor anything can harm us from without, unless we deserve it; unless we accept and believe that it is possible." We have already discussed this Truth, and once we know it and remember it, nothing can truly harm us.

We have not yet reached the point where we can sustain our bodies without taking in food, and the taste for meat, the need for its nutritional components only reflect our status as an omnivorous animal. Limiting ourselves to a vegetarian diet may not be unhealthy, but it's certainly no sign of spiritual elevation: Cattle are at the pinnacle of evolution for strict vegetarians. Put more simply, it takes more intelligence to hunt than to graze.

And that intelligence is more cleansing than dietary restriction. The higher studies, such as Metaphysics, help us to live in a more mental-spiritual world. The power of the mind can cleanse the cells of the body. The Principle of correspondence tells us, "As it is above, so it is below; as it is below, so it is above." Your mind unconsciously tells you what foods are best for you. And the time may well come when you find yourself eating less meat, or even find it distasteful to the point where you give it up voluntarily. This is all well and good; you have settled on a diet that will produce the best nutritional balance for your body's requirements—naturally, rather than by someone else's arbitrary decree.

When you study the Principle of Vibration, you will discover that it is indeed possible for a vibration of "lower frequency" to influence that of a greater one—as in the case of vibrations from killed animals—if the person is unaware of the Principle of Vibration, and believes that he can be so influenced. By his belief, he subjects himself to a law lower than himself, as Moses stated above.

These are only a few thoughts about the Commandment: "Thou shalt not kill," because you cannot kill. Life is positive, indestructible and eternal. Death is negative, an attempt to deny life. But it is no more than an attempt, for life is undeniable.

Thou Shalt not Steal

From reading the previous chapter, you already know the second or superior aspect of this Commandment: "You cannot steal." So there's no point in even thinking about it, much less trying. It simply can't be done. No one can rob you of that which belongs to you. They may try to; they may even manage to pick your pocket or burglarize your home. And, as long as you remain ignorant of the Law and believe you can be robbed, the missing possessions will be lost to you. But once you familiarize yourself with the law, repeat and remember its Truth, in one way or another your possessions will return to you, and no one will ever rob you again; in fact, you will never again, as long as you remain conscious of the Law, lose or misplace anything. You can prove it to yourself: The next time you cannot find something and consider it lost forever, repeat the law to yourself, and search again in this new light. You will find that you've thought of a new place to look, or you will search where you have already looked and find it, or you will remember circumstances under which you parted with it. This is one of the easiest lessons to learn.

Let's examine why nothing can be stolen. Your body contains within itself all of the elemental substances of our planet whether we refer to these fundamentally as earth, air, fire and water or the atomic elements from argon to zirconium. Furthermore, you are the sum of all the experience and knowledge of your chemical ancestry, from that first single-celled creature to the billions of specialized cells that make up your body today. On the cellular level, you have deeply buried memories of that first blind groping for food, the first struggle to take oxygen from air instead of water, those first steps as a thinking, planning biped. These memories are an inseparable part of you, far below the level of conscious recall—just as every cell in your body contains the genetic information needed to create an exact duplicate of your entire body—and none of this experience or information can ever be lost. And because this experience, this information is cumulative and unforgettable, you can truly never be diminished: Your spiritual evolution can never go backward, only forward. The Principle of Polarity tells us that like attracts like and opposites repel, thus we are attracted toward what we are growing to be and pushed on by what we have outgrown. Thus, with the start of every new life, learning the basics becomes easier and easier, because we are not learning, so much as remembering. By the time a child is born, he has already recapitulated his evolutionary history in the womb—first as a single cell, and on through a water-breathing then an air-breathing stage, until the final development of the complex cerebral cortex of the brain makes him ready to emerge as a human being. The child has already learned the primitive reflexes of hunger, discomfort, responses to sights and sounds. And many children, from their past experience, show remarkable abilities in certain areas: Mathematics, mechanics, athletic coordination, reading, the arts among others. The intelligent child, bored in the classroom, is simply frustrated at the time he must waste in relearning; though he may never seem to study, exams and conversation will prove that the learning is indeed there.

There is a multitude of evidence that reincarnation exists—but it's not mandatory. Free will exists for and in every creature. And just as people here on earth may either take advantage of an opportunity or pass it by, souls existing on the astral plane are free to return to earth, in order to continue their individual evolution, to acquire new experiences, repay old debts or reap the rewards of a good life—or to remain in the untroubled stasis of the higher plane. There is no authority to force a soul to return, only the individual desire to improve one's karma, which can only be achieved in the active, bustling physical world of changes.

Knowledge and experience are acquisitions which have been bought and paid for, acquired "by right of consciousness," which can neither be lost nor stolen, any more than any native ability or talent can be taken from you. Surprisingly, the same is true of material possessions, for they are the accompaniments of your earned abilities and deeds: Physical objects are earthly parallels of mental and spiritual gains; everything one has learned to use and enjoy, from the comforts of a palatial home to the utility of a simple book of matches, from jewelry to cutlery, remain ours in essence from incarnation to incarnation. So it may be said that those who are born wealthy have earned that wealth already—but it is still up to them to maintain that wealth, if they wish to keep it. Or they may "loose" it; perhaps as a means of improving their karma. As Jesus said: "Lay not up for yourselves treasures upon earth, where moth and rust do corrupt and where thieves break through and steal: But rather lay up for yourselves treasures in heaven, where neither moth nor rust do corrupt and no thieves break through and steal. For where your treasure is, there will your heart also be." (Matthew 6:19-21) Like all the proverbs of the Bible, this is significant on the material, mental and spiritual levels.

By now you understand that there is no need to live in fear of thieves. If you live in constant worry of robbery, being overcharged or embezzled from, you can now live in peace. And should something be taken from you, simply say to yourself the Truth: "Nothing that is mine by right of consciousness can be lost or stolen from me." Then forget the loss and be patient; soon someone will return the item to you, you will receive a gift to replace it or something of equal or greater value will come to you. What is earned cannot be taken from you. "Thou shalt not steal" because you cannot. And neither can anyone else.

But don't take my word for it. Use the thoughts and the treatments in this chapter to prove it to yourself.

Thou shalt not bear false witness

Many people wonder why there is no specific Commandment against lying, and then the Ninth Commandment covers the situation. In fact, all wrongdoing is a fundamental lie in that it contravenes the truth of harmony; and lies are covered more specifically in the first three Commandments, as we shall see later. The whole of the Commandments is an exposition of truth and a warning against every pretense and falsehood that mankind is heir to.

But, perhaps because of this lack of specific admonishment against lying in everyday life, man continues to distort the truth at his convenience. The commandment refers to the spoken or written word, that which "bears" the lie. The lie cannot truly exist, because there is only truth on all planes, and because the Law will return the appearance of the lie to you, to your detriment.

Election time, sad to say, is a prime example of human capacity for bearing false witness. We see parties and individuals publicizing statements of untruth and innuendo, and after the dust has settled, the winner begins his tenure secure in the belief that he has been recognized as the better man, whatever the truth or falsehood of his campaign claims. But he will be recognized by his actions, not his words—by his "fruits." Emerson said it well: "What you are shouts so loudly that I cannot hear what you have to say."

The Commandment says that what you see is your own conception of things. If you see beauty, it is a reflection of the beauty, the Truth within you. And if you see only ugliness, your words will reflect the falsehood within you—and you deny the reality that is Truth. And when you bear false witness, it is only testimony against yourself.

We have learned that the true self is perfect, having all the beauty of its Creator, since it was created by, with and from the essence of God. And this self, this being, is an expression of Truth—yours and that of everyone else; and when we display an attitude of ugliness, of falsehood, we display only ignorance of our own creative power, which is thought, or the recognition that ugliness cannot exist, lies cannot exist in the face of the Truth, which is all. Those who lie are not evil; they are but children who have yet to learn to recognize Truth.

When you give a small child modeling clay or crayons, you don't expect him to start churning out works that will rival those of Michelangelo (at least not for the first few weeks). You do expect a gradual learning process, as he gains the experience of discovering the limitations of his materials and his abilities, to learn by his mistakes and achievements—past and present. And he must learn to create what he sees. This is true of all of us, and if we want to change what we see, we must change our way of thinking about what we see.

Thus, you know that by recognizing falsehood for what it is, you project and establish Truth not only in your own eyes but also in those of others. By thinking and declaring the Truth, lies and misunderstandings begin to disappear. Truth is life and a lie is a hopeless attempt to negate truth. A lie has no life of its own and can only exist by virtue of the power you give it. And Truth is your source of power.

Your being or self is as perfect as everything else created by God; it is only the appearance of ugliness, wickedness, flaws and imperfections that you create for yourself. But since these are but illusions, you have only to deny them strongly, stating the Truth of your perfect essence—and the "false testimony" of your imperfection will begin to change for you and for all around you. The Truth has not changed: You have merely learned to recognize it, and have shown others your Truth by your example.

Truth can no more be changed than God can be offended. (We occasionally hear of man's actions being "an offense" to God. God cannot be offended or "hurt" by man. And nothing can mar or weaken a Principle. Can a fish change the currents of the sea?)

Thou shalt not covet

When an idea, a creation springs forth from the Divine mind, it already contains everything necessary for its complete development. It's inconceivable that God would send us an incomplete idea and allow us to frustrate ourselves trying to complete the puzzle. God is infinite wisdom, love and justice; He does not tease His children.

The universe is based on logic and order. The perfect harmony that exists in all its parts can be seen wherever we look, from the paths of the planets to the masterful engineering of an ant colony. Once this knowledge is acquired, we realize that nothing which is necessary is missing from our lives. When we have more than we need or want for our own happiness, it is there for the happiness of others.

Science says that "Nature abhors a vacuum" and this is demonstrably true. Even so-called empty space is crowded with dust motes and hydrogen clouds and random molecules drifting in their paths toward becoming something else.

Life is constantly searching for something to animate; this is its purpose. A small pot of earth left in any moist environment will soon host a stray seed and sprout forth. A forgotten glass of water will soon be swimming with larvae. Before a child is conceived, the womb is prepared to receive, nurture and protect the seed until it develops into a complete human being. The same is true of the eggs of birds, reptiles and insects, the seeds and spores of plant life. All contain the needs for the development of the complete creature. With man, completeness is fulfillment, and God has provided the seeds for this in every man. Therefore, a man can lack for nothing; everything has been foreseen, and has been made available.

And God completed the package by telling us, "Thou shalt not covet." In other words, that we have no need to envy or desire the possessions or good fortunes of another. Because we have but to ask for the things we want for ourselves. They are already ours. It is written in the Bible, "Ask and it shall be given unto you; seek and you shall find; knock and it shall be opened unto you." These are not idle words; they were meant to be taken seriously and literally. (Note that the idea was expressed three times.) The size of your desire, the scope of your dreams in general, is a measure of your need, and an indication of how close that need is to being fulfilled. Ask for what you want, and give thanks to God in the same breath. Do so without doubt, and you shall receive.

Your wish may come true through natural occurrences, through the generosity of a friend or as a miracle. (I remember an occasion when I was in New Orleans without a penny to my name. A transfer of funds had been late and it was a Saturday afternoon and the bank wouldn't be open until Monday—and I knew no one in the city. However, I knew the Truth and declared it, standing on the sidewalk: "My world contains everything: There is nothing missing in Creation. Father, I thank Thee, for I know Thou hast heard me." At that very moment, a green piece of paper was borne on the wind towards me and wrapped itself around my ankle. Knowing someone must have dropped it, I waited with that five-dollar bill in my hand to see if anyone was looking for it. No one was in sight; it was meant to be mine. It lasted me until Monday, with enough left over for a taxi ride to the bank, where my money was waiting. A miracle? Or a happy coincidence? I wonder if there's a difference.)

Miracles don't occur because a Principle has been violated, as many churches once believed, but by the proper action of that Principle.

We are applying that Principle by asking it to work in our behalf. A Principle cannot be altered. As one of my teachers said, "if the law of gravity were suspended to prevent a man from falling from a building, it wouldn't be a miracle, it would be chaos." If you look, you'll find that "logical explanation" behind every miracle. But what happens is still just as miraculous.

The First Commandment

The first three Commandments may be viewed as one, since they all refer to the nature of God. And, in fact, there is a difference of opinion between branches of Christianity as to whether these are three or four separate commandments. I have written them as one; the numbers here refer only to the text that follows.

(1) "I am the Lord thy God, which have brought thee out of the land of Egypt, out of the house of bondage. Thou shalt have no other gods before me."

(2) "Thou shalt not make unto thee any graven image, or any likeness of any thing that is in heaven above, or that is in the earth beneath or that is in the water under the earth."

(3) "Thou shalt not bow down thyself to them, nor serve them; for I the Lord thy God am a jealous God, visiting the iniquity of the fathers upon the children unto the third and fourth generation of them that hate me; and showing mercy unto the thousands of them that love me, and keep my commandments."

(4) "Thou shalt not take the name of the Lord thy God in vain; for the Lord will not hold him guiltless that taketh his name in vain."

* * *

In this Commandment, the phrase "The Lord Thy God" appears three times, signifying that it is to be taken literally on the material, mental and spiritual levels: He is the creator of all things; he is the supreme Law or Principle; he is that which dwells within us, the "higher self" that is one with God the Creator and God the Principle. These are three literal aspects of the one God.

Egypt is the symbol of earthly things, of the primitive man who has yet to reach the concept of a single, all-powerful and invisible God. The Egyptians worshiped many gods and bowed down before many graven images. There was one attempt to introduce monotheism to Egypt, on the part of Pharaoh Amenhotep (Akhnaten), but it was never accepted and died with him. Only Moses and his followers gave momentum to the new concept.

This is why (1) refers to Egypt and bondage, and commands: "Thou shalt have no other Gods before me." The earthly interpretation meant exactly what it said: That there was but one God, and that he forbade the creation of any other "gods" in any form. In (2) he stipulates such forms (similar to those of the Egyptians). And in (3) he clearly forbids the worship of such images, threatening punishment for this false worship and promising mercy for those who obey his Law.

To many in future generations, these words seemed almost childish, and they were reinterpreted, notably, by the prophet Ezekiel. The reluctance to accept the literal meaning of the words demonstrated the development of humanity over the generations.

Today, the symbolic meaning is clear: "I am God, who led you out of the bondage of materialism. I am the only source of all earthly and spiritual power; do not attribute such power to any other; do not shape images (in your mind) for the purposes of worshiping them; do not attempt to worship any thing or creature which is in your earthly experience (for I am invisible and these are but my creations). If you attempt these things, my Law will return your error to you, and to those you have taught to follow in your error; but if you follow in the Truth, the manifestations of your error will be corrected (I will bestow mercy on those who follow my commandments)."

Many of the Hebrews continued to take these words so literally that until recently there was no sign of any image in their synagogues; the same literalism in interpreting the Bible is true in many Christian denominations as well. The Levites so burdened themselves with the restrictions and impositions found in Leviticus that they could never fulfill the more than 600 requirements and rituals prescribed for daily existence; they condemned themselves to what they thought was failure in the eyes of God.

The Bible was never meant to be read this way. It is a psychological and metaphysical treatise, a book of Truth. It does not give orders; it explains, and provides advice for all circumstances of life on all levels of existence.

(4) "Thou shalt not take the name of the Lord thy God in vain" refers to errors we have already discussed. It means not to invoke the name of the Lord in asking for what you do not truly want. You do not really want God to damn another to hell. And if you ask it, you are only asking misfortune for yourself. You will not be "held guiltless" asking for such "favors." The Commandment also refers to your "name" as well, for on the higher plane, you are a part of God. You are not to abuse your own best interests with such phrases as "my bad memory," "my lousy luck," "my poor health" and so on. The law will not hold you guiltless—it will live up to your words, because they are decrees made in your name, the name of your higher self, which is of God.

Thou shalt not fornicate

I have changed this chapter heading from that in the table of contents of the original Ten Commandments to illustrate a point: That the words Moses handed down were also changed. The original was "Thou shalt not commit adultery." The same change was made in Matthew 19:9, probably by the same ecclesiastical zealots. It has been suggested that, at the time these changes were made, the word fornication referred only to adulterous activity; possibly this is so, but the change is still a gratuitous one.

Fornication refers to sexual activity while unmarried. Adultery refers to sexual activity on the part of married people outside of the marriage. (The Latin root is ad (to, by) + alter (other). This is, not so incidentally, the same basis for the word adulterate, meaning pollution or dilution by other materials. Which makes the insertion of this word into the Bible an adulteration itself.)

Note also that adultery in the Bible is often used in the sense of idolatry (worshiping another); this sense is also a part of the Commandment. It would have been impossible for a man as wise and enlightened as Moses, schooled as he was in hermetic Principles, to have instructed man to try and defy the Principle of Generation. The Principle works automatically on every plane. It is the same Principle which causes atomic attraction and the formation of molecules. The laws of attraction, cohesion and adhesion are integral parts of the Principle (as are gravity, magnetism and, on the atomic level, Strong Force and Weak Force). Without these forces, no matter would have existed above the level of the most basic subatomic particle: Attraction is the affinity of particle; adhesion is the "self determination" of the individual atom to accept or reject another atom or particle; cohesion is the ability of atoms to clump together. The strength of these laws is

given awesome expression in the energy required to split the atom—
and the energy given off when it happens.

The Principle is equally expressed among people, as is the Principle
of Correspondence ("As it is above, so it is below; as it is below, so it
is above.") Or, as the Kybalion says, "It is by studying the monad (the
most primitive unit of life) that one reaches the Angel."

Principles act automatically. The laws of adhesion and cohesion
among atoms might well be termed "fornication" between humans—
yet it is a process that goes on throughout the natural kingdoms. It's
as automatic as the bee's transmission of pollen from one flower to
another. Are we to presume that the Creator would hinder or prohibit
the processes He set in motion?

It's common knowledge that, by opposing a principle or force, we
multiply the force driving it. A dammed river will find another course,
or a lake will form, building up potential energy—the principle behind
hydroelectric power.

We are still of the animal kingdom; we still reproduce through
the sexual process. Perhaps we shall evolve beyond this stage of
development to a point where the Principle of Generation manifests
itself in another way, but we are still a long way from graduating to a
higher order of existence as a species.[2]

Revelation also states that the Lord announced that at this time of
evolution, "No more children will be born." Perhaps we are entering

---

2 Students often ask, when presented with this concept, if we all evolved at once, what
would happen to the human race? The answer lies in your point of view. We would
still be "we," whatever our state of being. And another evolving species might
well come up to fill the gap, and call themselves "humanity." There will always be
someone at the lower levels. This is one level of meaning in Jesus' saying, "The
poor, you shall always have with you." He meant not only the economically poor,
but the underdeveloped in knowledge, experience and evolution as well.

that phase even now, for, though population is increasing at an incredible rate, birth rates will soon start to decline.

Another description of this evolutionary era was given by Jesus as, "When the veil of shame falls"—that is when we realize that shame is artificial, that all the "veil" (which is ignorance) can hide is Truth, and when Truth is universally known, we will be ready for that evolutionary "graduation."

A perfect example of that "veil" of ignorance is the erroneous use of the word fornication. By focusing so much attention on the natural, we have made it seem unnatural; in effect, we have tried to oppose the Principle of Generation, and it simply can't be done. By stemming that river, we have caused it to seek other channels, and we have produced mental aberrations, sexual deviations, frustration, dishonor, shame and punishment. Much of it due to the arbitrary substitution of a single word.

Bonsai trees, small and twisted, have their beauty as curiosities. But they are still distortions of what was meant to be, stunted versions of what they might have been, without intervention, as are the caged bird, the chained leopard, the gelded stallion. We have modified Truth and modified the Scriptures out of ignorance, or to gain power over others.

Metaphysically, the meaning of "Thou shalt not commit adultery" is "Thou shalt not misinterpret or misapply the Law." Because you will not be able to; because your attempt to do so will only bring misery back on yourself. The Commandment refers to that very fanaticism through which it has been, itself, misinterpreted.

To Jesus, that fanaticism was more repulsive, more deserving of punishment than unfettered sexuality. As he expressed it: "Woe unto thee, Chorazin, woe unto thee Bethside; for it shall be more tolerable for Tyre and Sidon at the Judgment than for thee." Chorazin and

Bethside were the centers of religious Zealotry and fanaticism in those days, while Tyre and Sidon were known for their sexual profligacy. Thus, He was saying that fanaticism was far more punishable in the eyes of the Lord than sexual transgressions.

What about adultery in the strict sense? Let's go back to Matthew 19:3-12. "The Pharisees also came unto him, tempting him, and saying unto him, is it lawful for a man to put away (divorce) his wife for every cause? And he answered and said unto them, Have ye not read, that he which made them at the beginning made them male and female? And said, For this cause shall a man leave his father and mother and shall cleave unto his wife, and the twain shall be one flesh? What therefore God hath joined together, let no man put asunder."

"They said unto him, why did Moses then command to give a writing of divorcement and to put her away? He saith unto them, Moses, because of the hardness of your hearts suffered you to put your wives away: But from the beginning it was not so. And I say unto you, whosoever shall marry another, ((except it be for fornication)) committeth adultery: And whosoever marrieth her that is put away doth commit adultery."

The double parentheses above indicate the post-scriptural "adulteration" I referred to earlier, Christ did not believe that two wrongs make a right.

"His disciples say unto him, If the case of a man be so with his wife, it is not good to marry. But he said unto them, All men cannot receive this saying, save they to whom it is given. For there are some eunuchs which were so born from their mother's womb: And there are some eunuchs made eunuchs by other men; and there be eunuchs which have made themselves eunuchs for the kingdom of heaven's sake. He that is able to receive it, let him receive it."

The "case" referred to is abstention from sexual activity, whether from physical or psychological impotence or by choice. Christ's answer here is that, if they choose to marry, the two are still "one flesh" in at least the spiritual sense. And that is the sense that counts. The Principle of Generation is still active, in the laws of attraction, adhesion and cohesion. If a woman seeks gratification outside the marriage because of this situation, is this adultery? Technically and physically, yes. But is it an exception to the rule? No. And Christ implies that this is none of our business, that it is between the man and wife. Some people can handle the situation, some cannot: "He that is able to receive it let him receive it."

Now let's go back to the metaphysical side of the question. There is a balance in the sexes, in that there is, indeed, a "man" for every "woman," for these are two halves of a spiritual "cell"—they are created as one and indivisible. On the earthly plane, they are separate beings, but the original attraction is unavoidable. On earth there is a constant search for one's other half—but even if that search is fruitless, the two will ultimately be joined in the spiritual realm.

This is encouraging news for people who are lonely, or who have made the wrong match—to know that other perfect half is waiting. And if we find that match on earth, no power on earth can separate them. We have met and joined our true partners in past lives, and it is that memory that kindles our continuous search for him or her.

Society has clung to the saying "That which God has joined together, let no man put asunder." But it has been misinterpreted as a reference to marriage—which is a civil or religious ceremony—and not to that true spiritual union forged by God, which the marriage may or may not represent. This saying is not an indictment of divorce, which is simply another human convenience, but a consolation, offered by a loving God, telling us that, whatever else happens, that true union still exists, and cannot be severed.

Jesus spoke in parables, stories in which the meaning was clear in the situation, not merely in the words, which he knew would suffer in translation, or even in repetition. The words might change, but the story, the metaphor, does not.

Jesus' reference to the eunuch is parabolic. It can be taken in the literal sense and still be seen for the analogy which it is. His reference to eunuchs "for the kingdom of heaven's sake" refers to those who have chosen to channel their human energies, including the sexual drive, into a dedication to the studies that will help them evolve toward a higher being, even in this earthly environment. This is the basis for the justification of a celibate priesthood. As Jesus said, "He that is able to receive it, let him receive it."

This is one Commandment that scholars and ecclesiastics are most reluctant to discuss. Even Jesus was a bit cryptic, couching his answers in parable form. The reason is that we are still earthbound animals, barely into a true mental state. There is conflict within us between pure reason and our instincts and drives, and maintaining a balance is most difficult. Let us remember the real meaning of the commandment: That we cannot commit adultery. And if, in trying, we bring hurt to another, that hurt will come back to us.

Let us also remember the time when a woman, caught in adultery, was brought before Jesus, according to the laws of Israel, she should have been stoned to death. Jesus stooped and wrote idly in the earth at his feet. They continued to ask his opinion and he responded: "He that is without sin among you, let him cast the first stone at her." Again he stooped and wrote in the earth. When he looked up, the woman stood alone. He asked her, "Woman, where are those thine accusers? Hath no man condemned thee?" She answered "No man, Lord." And Jesus said to her: "Neither do I condemn thee: Go and sin no more."

Recommendation

*A*ny book on metaphysics should be read many times. Every re-reading brings better understanding. Repetition is the basis of the treatments described in these pages, because only that which is practiced remains with us. What is read once and is not used, disappears.

Book II

Your Heart's Desire

The Secret Conny Méndez
Discovered over 70 Years Ago

Conny Méndez discovered *The Secret* more than 70 years ago and then she wrote this book with her traditional positive style, looking for prosperity and without forgetting what is most important: the spiritual content.

This book, *Your Heart's Desire* (*Te regalo lo que se te antoje,* Caracas, Venezuela 1969) is nothing but the same secret, summarized and adapted for the English language in common, everyday words that will respond to many needs of the human being.

To understand the teachings of the New Age and fully realize the benefits it offers, it is recommended to read this book. Here, the correct way to pray for love, life, death, voice of your soul, success and well-being among others, is explained.

THE PUBLISHERS

Introduction

This book will help you to realize your goals in life, both immediate and long-range. In order to make the fullest and most effective use of this volume, however, I strongly urge that you read my book, *Metaphysics for Everyone,* which is easily available. This book provides the foundations on which this series is built, beginning with the Principle of Mentalism—the principle by which everything in Creation functions at its highest level. Without the basic knowledge contained in this first book, the principles used here cannot be fully understood, and may cause unneeded confusion.

This series began as a program of free lectures, but it soon became obvious that the audience for these studies in New Age Awareness was far vaster than the capacity of any auditorium yet built, and so I have revised and expanded the lectures into a printed format for the benefit of an international audience.

Read these books. Practice their principles with confidence. You will begin to reap the benefits and rewards you want sooner than you expect.

And, above all, share this knowledge with others. The Universe is vast enough to encompass every "Heart's Desire"!

CONNY MÉNDEZ

CARACAS, 1969

Getting Started.
No Time Like the Present

1. *T*ake a piece of paper—or several—and write down, in order of importance, all the things you wish for. Don't be concerned about having too many wishes, or wishing for too much. The Power you will be calling upon knows no limits. (Fairy tales usually limit their protagonists to a standard "three wishes"—but the boundaries of reality are not so stifling!)

2. Read your list every morning when you wake up and every night before going to sleep. Just as writing down your desires crystalizes your thinking, reading what you have written focuses your mind on what you want.

3. Think about your wishes. Often. Enjoy imagining them as realities. Everyone enjoys such daydreaming—but most people's daydreams are vague and unstructured. Yours will have strength and solidity—because every time you think about your wishes, you will say; "Thank you, Father, for I know that you have already arranged for my wishes to be granted."

4. Do not tell anyone what you are doing. This is most important, because the more people you tell at this stage of things, the more you dilute the power you are using. (Much of that power lies in your own belief, your own knowing that this process works. Telling others invites their skepticism, which can gnaw at the underpinnings of your belief, at this early stage.) There will be time enough for sharing later—after your wishes start becoming realities.

These are the basic techniques, the active side of the process. The rest of the procedure—its real strength—is a matter of attitude. A businessman might call this "conscious goal orientation." And he'd be right—except that it soon becomes subconscious, and even more positive and powerful.

Be good to yourself. Be generous in your wishes. Don't write down on your list that you'd like "a new home—nothing fancy, just a nice little cottage" when what you have in mind is more along the lines of a Mediterranean villa. Be honest. (But remember, there's a balance that must be struck. That honesty has to work both ways. Don't casually wish for a reproduction of the Palace at Versailles unless you have serious plans for founding a small principality or harbor a secret desire to operate the world's most luxurious resort. Besides -- would you really want all the headaches and responsibilities of running an estate of that size? In other words, keep your wishes in line with your capacity to enjoy their fulfillment!) The same common sense applies whether you are wishing for money, a career, a change of locale.

When you make out your first list, keep it simple. Put down your most immediate and urgent goals first. You'll find that they will lead in the direction of your long-range goals automatically. You'll find yourself editing and rewriting your list with surprising regularity— particularly as your requests are answered and your horizons begin to expand. And you'll find yourself crossing off some wishes, either because they have been granted, or because they are no longer important as your values change.

Another reason for keeping your early list simple is to allow yourself to focus on it more clearly, and to become accustomed to actually experiencing the realization of your wishes. At this stage, you simply won't believe your wishes can come true. And here I must warn you that doubt is your worst enemy. It may be the most natural feeling in the world at this point to be skeptical of a new idea, particularly one that sounds too good to be true. But you must learn to push doubt aside, and when you have such feelings, simply take out your list, review it and give thanks once more. Do it aloud: The sound of your own words will help to break the skeptical chains that can hold you back. What can be a more positive expression of belief than giving thanks for something not yet received? If you recall the story of the Loaves and the Fishes, you may remember that Jesus, faced with the prospect of feeding 5,000 followers with only five loaves of bread and five fishes, simply looked up and gave thanks before breaking the first loaf. I can think of no better example to follow.

So, prepare yourself to be surprised almost every time you consult your list... to discover that you'll have to cross out some wishes, since they've already been granted (sometimes subtly, as part of another wish) or rendered unnecessary because of other changes in your life. You'll find yourself rewriting often, making new wishes, rewording others to remove ambiguity, changing their order of importance. This is a very natural part of the process; everyone goes through it. What is happening is simply that your higher Self (or Ego, if you prefer) is itself undergoing changes; you'll begin realizing how many of these wishes are already within your reach or just a little way down the road.

One caution: Don't start dictating just exactly how and when your wishes are to manifest themselves. This can delay or even halt their progress. You are tapping a great spiritual Force, which, though it is subject to human control under the right conditions, is far beyond human understanding. Do not attempt to interpret or second-guess its actions—simply accept the results with gratitude. Above all, do not make the mistake of thinking, "This can't have happened just because I wished for it—it must have been meant to happen anyway." This is deterministic doubt, and as an attitude can cripple your further efforts. Remember, this great Force (known in Metaphysics as the Law of Precipitation) is totally impersonal. It makes no judgments, but follows the channels already in existence in your life to fulfill your desires in the simplest, most natural and harmonious ways. It is almost never a display of fireworks—the out-of-the-blue inheritance from the uncle you never heard of. Instead it is subtle: You may find yourself crossing a wish off your list because it had been granted long before you wished it, but you simply hadn't recognized it for what it was, or because that wish was always within your reach -- or because it's simply no longer important to you. The Law fulfills its function in the way that is most beneficial to you.

Ask and it shall be given you; seek and ye shall find; knock and it shall be opened unto you.

MATTHEW. VII, 7.

The Master Key

You will find in the pages to come that I often quote and refer to the ideas of Dr. Emmet Fox. My admiration and affection toward him as my teacher and mentor is one reason. The other is that he was—and is, though he is no longer among us in physical form—a master in the art of "getting out of trouble." And getting out of trouble is the most immediate and visible way of bettering one's life—as anyone who has ever been subjected to illness, legal problems, joblessness or poverty will be quick to agree. In this regard, Dr. Fox writes:

"I have condensed my essay as much as possible. I wish I could have done it in only one or two lines. It isn't an instructive writing; it is simply a formula to get you out of trouble. Studying is well and good in its proper place and proper moment, but it will not solve your problems. Only by working to raise and transform your awareness of things will the manifestation of a problem either cease or fix itself correctly.

"The Master key is awareness through Scientific Prayer. But awareness—which must be an objective state -- cannot be achieved in the face of subjective involvement. For the benefit of those who have yet to experience the greatest Power in the universe, the suggestions that follow are designed to bring you into touch with that Power, and to produce results you can believe in."

First, bear in mind that God is omnipotent and that humankind is made in His image and likeness. This is the claim of the Spiritual Doctrine, and it should be taken not literally, but quite seriously. The Power—God's own omnipotence—is not solely the prerogative of a saint or a mystic. It exists for and is available to all human beings. Whoever, wherever you are, this awareness is the Master Key to Harmony. And through Scientific Prayer, you allow God's power to work to your benefit—but He is the one to act, not you. Your only function is to remove your emotional self from the picture, so that you may better serve as a channel, unobstructed by subjectivity, for God's will to act upon your wishes. If you can achieve this objective "sidestep," none of your defects or limitations will obstruct the process. Nor does it matter what your religion may be. You are God's creation, and that is sufficient.

Here's how it works: Whenever you find yourself in a dilemma, do not think about it. Instead, think about God. Concentrate on what you know and believe about him: That He is all-powerful, all-wise and ever-present; That He is infinite love, wisdom and truth. Do not think about the problem, but about the solution, which is God. Put the problem aside, along with yourself. You have placed your problem in the most capable hands in the universe: Those that created the universe, and that problem will be resolved in accordance with His Law of Harmony, to your complete satisfaction. Don't try to predict, to interfere, or to second-guess His methods. It's not your problem any more.

The Effective Way to Pray

*T*he spiritual approach to any problem is achieved by raising your thoughts, your consciousness, above the level of the problem. If you are able to accomplish this, the problem will solve itself. Metaphysically speaking, it's analogous to "getting out of your own way." The more difficult the problem—i.e., the deeper it is buried in your subconscious—the higher you must elevate your thought processes. A small problem, such as the irritation of a parking-lot dent in your car, or uncalled for rudeness from a stranger, can be handled by telling yourself to be objective about it—by treating the problem to a mental shrug. (A practice quite accurately referred to as "rising above the situation.")

The difference between minor and serious or even life threatening problems is simply a matter of degree. But practicing on the smaller problems makes your approach to the larger ones that much easier.

It's not a matter of rearranging your thoughts about the problem. In fact, conscious thought about a situation is to be avoided: The object is to remove yourself from the problem, to achieve a higher level of awareness. Turn your thoughts instead to a contemplation of the spiritual facts of life. What are the conditions of the Spiritual world? How does God manifest Himself? How does your own higher consciousness manifest itself? The answer to all these questions lies in the word perfection. The conditions of the Spiritual Universe are perfection. God shows himself in that perfection. And the higher you can rise in your thoughts, the closer you come to achieving that perfection: The absence of disease, strife, poverty, death, ugliness, war and evil. When you can "see" this condition, so opposite to that which you see manifested on the physical plane, it will begin to transform that spiritual truth into physical fact.

Jesus achieved his miracles—curing the ill, reforming sinners, controlling storms and raising the dead—through his ability to raise his consciousness as high as needed to accomplish the miraculous. (You may feel that Jesus had a considerable advantage, considering his parentage—but you must remember that we share that parentage, as children of God!)

What, then, is true prayer, effective prayer? Simply stated, it is a meditation on the perfection that is the spiritual world, and which can be the physical world. It can be contemplation of God, of beauty, of words on a page. There are those who have achieved this higher state by merely repeating "God is Love" until the words ceased to have meaning—and then took on new and truer meaning. (The same principle as the Indian mantra: Repetition that opens the mind.) Others have found inspiration by reading metaphysical writings, or the Bible itself—relying on the metaphysical Principle of Attraction to guide their hands and eyes to the right passages. Whatever method you may choose—and you may feel free to come up with your own—there are only two important "musts": You must forget your problems and you must forget yourself.

Effective prayer is the awareness of spiritual perfection. And the stronger that awareness, the stronger the influence perfection will have on your life.

God and Business

*B*usiness is simply a matter of negotiations between people. Buying, selling; looking for a job or looking for an employee; whether it's a household item at a garage sale or a contract between multinational corporations, the principle remains the same—and the results must be satisfactory to both parties. It's a matter of give and take until an agreeable balance is achieved. Dr. Emmet Fox refers to the process as looking for and finding God on both sides of the fence.

And God is on both sides. Because both sides are His, and His only concern is to create a balance, a harmony of points of view between His children.

So don't try to impose your point of view on the other party. Be aware that God is the only one in charge of the situation, that His will is at play on both sides, and that His will is the harmony of mutual benefit. Simply state your objectives and views clearly and honestly. Discard the old habit of assuming that the other party is out to take you for all he can. Just consider that he wants to benefit from this negotiation as much as you do, and remember that God lives within him as He does within you, and proceed with complete fairness.

Don't exaggerate your abilities or overstate your case. Don't try to convince the other party that his point of view is wrong. Concentrate on pointing out where his viewpoint and yours meet. And don't try too hard. If you don't get this job or employee, this sale or acquisition, it may well mean that there's a better one down the road. Above all, take it easy. On the spiritual plane, everything is easier than it looks.

And, as always, state your wish for the outcome, and give thanks in advance: "According to God's will, in harmony and perfection, I wish (...) I thank you, Father, for I know You have heard me."

The Power of Verbalization

*T*he word, particularly the spoken word, has a power all its own. It concentrates and focuses thoughts and beliefs. The prayer that follows is in my own words. I urge you to take the thoughts it expresses, put them into words you are comfortable with, and say them aloud whenever you wish to rise above the problems of the day. When these thoughts have become truth to you, you will have begun to elevate your consciousness, and true prayer—effective prayer—will have begun:

I AM Divine Spirit. I live, move, think and have all
my being in God. I AM part of God's expression, and
so I express perfect harmony. I AM a personification
of omniscience. I possess direct knowledge of Truth. I
possess perfect intuition. I possess spiritual perception.
I know.

God is my wisdom, so there is no room for error. God
is my intelligence, so I can only reason correctly. There
is no time lost because time is God's creation. God
acts through me, so I can only act correctly, and pray
correctly. Therefore I will always think the right thing,
at the right time, in the right way. My work will always
come out well, because it is God's work. The Holy
Spirit is my inspiration. My thoughts are fresh, clear
and powerful, for they come from the omnipotence of
God. My prayers come from the spirit of God; they are

as powerful as the eagle, as docile and as simple as the dove. They are uttered in the name of God Himself and so they cannot come back to me without fulfillment. All I wish for will be granted and I will prosper in all my wishes. I thank God for this.

What is Love?

*D*r. Emmet Fox has recommended the next four passages:

God is love, and he who dwells in love dwells in God, and God in him.

I JOHN. IV, 16.

***

Love is the most important feeling of all. It is the golden door to Paradise. Ask for understanding in love and meditate on it daily. Banish all fear. Love is the Fulfillment of the whole Law; it covers a multitude of sins and it is totally invincible.

***

There is no problem, no difficulty that cannot be overcome with love. There is no illness that cannot be cured with enough love. There is no door that will not open in the face of enough love, nor is there any abyss that cannot be crossed with enough love. There is no barrier that enough love cannot tear down, and there is no sin so great that it cannot be forgiven with enough love.

***

No matter how deeply one is mired in error, how desperate a situation, how great a mistake or how overwhelming a problem... if you are able to love enough, you shall be the most powerful and happiest being on Earth.

The Presence

*T*he following is one of the strongest affirmative statements/ meditations/prayers which can be used in achieving the elevation of your consciousness. Read it to yourself until its meaning is clear, and then speak it aloud:

God is the only Presence and the only Power that exists. God is with me at this moment and forever. God is all, and all that is not God exists only in shadow. God is the Perfect Good; He is the only Cause of Perfect Good. God never sends illnesses, accidents, temptations or death; nor does He authorize these conditions. God, who is the Perfect Good, creates only good. Salt water and fresh cannot spring from the same fountain.

I myself am Divine spirit, for I AM a child of God. I move with God; I live with and of God, therefore I AM not afraid. I AM surrounded by God's peace, and all is harmony. I do not fear people; I do not fear circumstances; I do not fear myself, for I AM of God. God's peace fills my soul and fear cannot brush me with even the lightest of touches. I do not fear the past; I do not fear the present; I do not fear the future, because God is with me. The Eternal Father abides within and around me and His loving arms are always open to receive me. Nothing will ever touch me unless it comes from God, and God is Love.

God is Life. I fully understand this and express it. God is Truth. I fully understand this and express it. God is Divine Love. I fully understand this and express it. I send only thoughts of love to the Universe; to all things that live and grow; to all animals that walk, crawl, swim or fly; to all people, every man, woman and child on this earth, with no distinction whatsoever. If anyone has harmed me or done me wrong, I voluntarily and totally forgive that person and the matter is closed forever. I forget and let go. I AM free and those I have forgiven are free as well. If there is any resentment left within me, I ignore it; it will wither and crumble to dust to be blown away by the breath of the Spirit, and I AM forever free.

God is infinite Wisdom and that Wisdom is mine. It guides me and shows me the way and I shall not be led into error. His Light is a lamp unto my feet. God is infinite Life and that Life is my substance and my being. I shall lack for nothing. God created and sustains me; His Divine Love has provided for all my needs and wants. There is only one Mind, only one Power, only one Principle, only one Being, and only one God. He is closer to me than my own limbs, than my own breath.

I AM Divine Spirit. I AM a child of God and I shall live in His presence all my days. I thank my creator for this perfect harmony.

A Verbal Approach to
Developing Divine Love

*T*he two all-too-accessible keys that open the doors to Hell are criticism and resentment—commonly expressed as anger. But they can be obliterated permanently by speaking the words below.

Love is not merely a feeling of affection for another person. It manifests itself in many forms, and one of the highest forms is universal love—not an emotion directed at a single person, but an all-encompassing expression of goodwill and forgiveness, a constant broadcast radiating good thoughts to all others.

To seek God is to love Him. To try to purify our thoughts is to love God. To try to correct misunderstandings is to love our neighbors, which is loving God. To love beauty and art is to love the creations of God and man, which is to love God. All love is the Love of God. Divine love, reflected upon its Creator and Embodiment.

There is no fear in Love. For Love destroys all fear. Fear torments, and whoever is tormented by fear has not yet perfected Love.

The prayer meditation that follows will help you develop your capacity for Divine Love:

My soul is full of Divine Love and I AM surrounded by that Love. I project Love and Goodwill for all. I possess conscious Divine Love. God is Love, and there is nothing in all creation that is not God or of God. All human beings are expressions of Divine Love; therefore all I meet can only be such manifestations of His Love.

This is the only Truth. This is my reality, the reality of all things in my life. I do not need to force my perception of facts and events into a mold for this to be true: I see this Truth in all things at all times. God's Divinity is the nature of all beings. There is but one all-pervasive Divine Love and I AM fully conscious of it.

I understand perfectly what Divine Love is, because I AM a conscious manifestation of its presence. God's love burns in me for all humanity; I extend God's love to all whom I meet, to all of whom I think.

I forgive all that needs to be forgiven by me without exception. I AM filled with Divine Love, and all is in perfect order. I radiate love to the universe and to all that dwell therein. I experience Divine Love; I manifest Divine Love. I thank my Creator for this Truth.

Fifteen Parameters

Are you on the right path to Harmony and to the fulfillment of your heart's desires? You are if you can honestly state the following:

• I always seek the Good in each person, thing or situation.

• I resolutely turn my back on the past, good or bad, and live exclusively for the present and the future.

• I forgive all people without exception for whatever they may have done. I forgive myself for whatever I may have done—for if I cannot forgive (love) myself, I can never truly forgive (love) another.

• I look at my daily work as a sacred task, and try to fulfill my duties to the best of my ability, and to find joy in that fulfillment, no matter how troublesome those duties may be.

• I do everything in my power to maintain a healthy body and to create a harmonious environment around me.

• I try to be of service to others, and to do so without meddling or becoming bothersome.

• I unconditionally avoid adverse criticism, refusing to offer it, to listen to it or encourage it.

• I try to make the Truth known at every opportunity, subtly, discreetly: I do so not by preaching, but through the example of my own well-being.

• I dedicate at least fifteen minutes a day to meditation and prayer.

• I read at least seven verses from the Bible or a chapter from any appropriate book which speaks of the Truth of this Era.

• I make a special prayer or meditation each day to reaffirm my knowledge or ask for greater understanding that God is with all humankind and me.

• I train myself to give my first thought upon waking to God.

• I set aside a few moments every day for "Silent Radiation"—that is letting my thoughts spread the word of Love throughout the Universe. (During exercise, upon awakening, or at any set time during the day.)

• I put the Golden Rule into practice at all times, instead of merely respecting and admiring it. I do unto others as I would have them do unto me, whether they reciprocate or not. (This rule has its reciprocal as well: I do not allow others to do to me what I would not do to them.)

• I AM fully aware that the conditions which face me are as fleeting as mirages, and that I can change any situation for the better through the power of scientific prayer.

My World Holds Everything

*H*ow many times have you found that something you need to continue what you are doing is missing? A button missing from the shirt you're putting on… a pen when you need to jot something down… the right size wrench when you're stuck under the car. In realizing something's missing, you are only seeing half of the picture: The physical situation. The Truth lies in the Spiritual Plane, and the Truth involves the solution as well as the situation, for only then is the situation complete. You must connect with the Spiritual, and ask, "what is the True situation?" And, if you have been following the procedures in this book, the answer will come back: "Perfection." And your mind will fill the gap. It may be another shirt you'd forgotten about which is just as appropriate, a pen handed you by a friend, or found in another pocket, a wrench mislaid but still within reach, or someone happening by who can quickly hand it to you. These are the commonplace solutions to commonplace problems, but they illustrate the Spiritual approach.

The Truth is that nothing is missing. Not ever.

Think of it this way: Your body is generic to the plane it occupies. It contains all the elements that can be found in other beings and objects on this same plane. The same is true of your Spiritual self. It is composed of thought and memory; the memories of this life, immediately at hand, and the unconscious memories of past lives, which manifest themselves as intuition, instinct and awareness. Your Spiritual self is generic to its plane—wherein lies all experience, all solutions, completeness, perfection.

Therefore, once you have elevated your thoughts to the spiritual level, you have the complete authority to say, "My world contains everything I can ever need; therefore I can lack nothing. Spiritually, everything is at hand, and I now claim its material manifestation in such a way as to fill my needs on the physical plane." Wait a moment, and a small miracle will occur. A miracle as mundane as the problem it solves: That forgotten other shirt, or the appearance of someone who can sew on a matching button in two minutes.

Naturally, you'll be saying to yourself, "I can take care of the little stuff—what about real problems?"

The answer remains the same: You will never in this existence be deprived of anything you truly need. Elevating your thoughts to the level of effective prayer, as described above, will open the door to your solutions on the physical plane. If there is a financial problem, a job, a gift, a loan or some way to get out of the problem will present itself. If the problem is medical, prayer will bring the answer. And, more often than not, that answer will be to follow the advice of your physician, though you may find yourself drawn to a change in diet or habit patterns. Most often, the answer will come in a change of attitude as well. An attitude that says, "There is no reason for me to be ill. I AM creating a healthy spiritual self; and my healthy soul will keep my physical body in perfect health as well." If it is a problem of the heart, elevating your thoughts above that problem will bring you the serenity to see the solution that awaits you.

As an extreme example, people have said, "O.K., what if I'm in the middle of a desert, dying of thirst, and there's no water to be had?" Scientific Prayer brings extreme measures to solve extreme problems. The spiritual plane holds memories of this life and all precious lives. Knowledge such as the signs that indicate water only a few feet under the sand, the nearness of moisture-bearing cacti. A loved one, or even a chance acquaintance may have initiated a search. An oasis or highway may lie over the next dune. These are all possibilities. But the real answer to such extremes is that, once you are accustomed to dealing with the problems of everyday life through effective prayer, such extreme problems simply do not arise; this is because prayer and awareness create a pattern in your life, and part of that pattern is the automatic avoidance of situations that could lead to such extreme circumstances.

Many of the answers that come to you will be common-sense ones. Many will be the solutions you already knew were available to you, but that you had, for some reason, avoided or ignored. And some will truly appear to be miracles, small or large. The point is that true, effective prayer opens your awareness and brings those solutions to you when you need them. You will become one of those people others refer to as "lucky"—but the fact is, you have created your own "luck" through Scientific Prayer!

The Bogeyman

*E*veryone's heard of the "bogeyman"[3], that imaginary ogre of childhood. But we all outgrow believing in that monstrous figure as adults—or do we?

Maybe we stop believing in that particular personification or dread, but all we do is substitute for it any number of other fears and worries—over things that do not exist.

You may remember back to when you were somewhere between three and seven years old, when someone told you about the Bogeyman, and how he was going to "get you" some dark night. (The authoritative source of this knowledge may have been an equally frightened peer, hoping to diminish his own fear by sharing it, a somewhat sadistic older child, who had just outgrown his own belief in such things, or a misguided parent, striving for discipline. Whatever the source, belief comes easily to a very young, open and grasping mind.) But you probably remember your heart pounding so hard you could hear it, the chills that ran down your spine, the wobbly knees and an overwhelming desire to burrow a good half a mile under the bed covers.

In fact, you may remember those feelings from the last time you were pulled over for a traffic violation, or the time you had to stand up and speak before a group of strangers, or when you find yourself looking down twenty stories over a balcony railing that seems too

---

3 Bogeyman (or less commonly bogyman) a monstrous imaginary figure used in threatening children. [Merriam-Webster. (N.D.). Bogeyman. In Merriam-Webster. com dictionary. Retrieved April 9, 2020, from https://www.merriam-webster.com/dictionary/bogeyman]. *Ed.*

low and too flimsy. You've cast aside the Bogeyman and substituted a basketful of new ones, fears that may seem more real and "adult" but are in fact just as imaginary and groundless.

Dr. Emmet Fox, in an article "dedicated to people with worries," says: "I never scold someone who is worried. This would be like kicking someone when he's down. Do you think a person worries because he has nothing better to do? Of course, there are people who are forever complaining; they seem to enjoy feeling sorry for themselves and having people listen to their imaginary problems. This is not a normal attitude, and one that probably needs professional help, but it certainly does not fall into the category of a real worry."

The real worry is something that nags at its victim, a living hell from which the victim experiences tremendous relief whenever the smallest solution shows itself. Worry about having more bills than money to pay them; about a lawsuit that may well be decided against you; about a loved one's illness, or your own; about a wrong you have done someone, or one someone has done you; about the love you feel for someone who does not return it—or vice-versa. In the physical world, these are justifiable causes for concern.

But, in the spiritual world, all worries are "imaginary." There is no more reason to fear a court judgment against you than there is for an agoraphobic to fear open spaces. On this plane, problems exist only because you believe they exist. You give your problems life—and you can put and end to them. With Scientific Prayer, you can do the same thing to these "bogeymen" that you did to your childhood demon: Disbelieve them. Once you have elevated your thoughts and spoken a Prayer of Perfection, problems will begin to be replaced by solutions, and worries by serenity. It probably won't happen immediately. It may take days, weeks, even months, but, once you have firmly established your belief in the spiritual perfection that is God's universe, that perfection will begin to manifest itself on the physical plane.

The Truth is that the physical plane is not the real one, not the fixed, immutable "reality" we thought it was. Our material or physical situations are nothing more than the outward reflections of our minds' convictions, and since we have the power to change these convictions, we have the power to alter the outward manifestations, whenever we really try to. This is the real power of prayer.

Now you understand why I say that there is no need for worry. Because even "real" worries aren't real after all. Not when you can consider what seems to be a total disaster and tell yourself that you can, by adopting the right attitude and by developing the ability to elevate your thoughts to the level of Scientific Prayer, change the situation into something entirely different. When you feel, believe, know this to be true, you can safely say that all worries have been and will be eliminated from your life, and it will be only a matter of time before your health, your prosperity, your inner harmony will become permanent situations in your life.

And you will have laid all the "bogeymen" that have plagued your life to rest forever.

Money

*P*rofessor Fillmore, the founder of Unity, says: "It isn't a crime to be rich, and there is no virtue whatsoever in being poor, as all the reformers would have us believe. What is bad is to accumulate wealth without allowing it to circulate freely so that it also reaches the needy. If we all were to have what is referred to as the conscience of poverty, then abject poverty, as we see it in India and Africa, would be worldwide.

"There, all those millions of people are forever tied down by the conditioning of poverty, they suffer lack, in every shape and form, from birth to death. The thoughts of the impoverished echo back to the Earth, to the soil, and so, year after year, the crop yield is poor, and thousands die of hunger."

What we need to develop is prosperity conditioning. We begin by discarding all the old and false concepts of "lack," of "doing without," of dependence on fixed patterns. The idea that something is too expensive depends on how empty or full our pockets are. We make a comparison between the cost of an item and the amount of money at hand. If our resources are limited, the item seems too expensive. If our resources are healthy, we don't give a thought to the price and simply buy it. It is not the item itself that is "reasonable" or "too expensive," it is our thinking that is "poor."

Sure, there are plenty of things that are overpriced. But, if you had plenty of money, they wouldn't really seem so outrageous. You'd find yourself saying that you're really paying for quality, a better fit, and the reliability of a major brand name. So, it's really not the cost but the state of your finances that stands in your way. And all that hinges on the state of your consciousness.

From the time when we were very small, most of us who were not born to wealth have heard the subject of money mentioned at home—what things cost and what was beyond the family's reach. Very few of us were able to ask for anything we wanted and get it without hesitation. Instead, we heard, "That's much too expensive," or, "We just don't have the money." Even though we weren't starving, or lacking for the basics of life, we were still subjected to an early pattern of "poverty conditioning."

How do we break that conditioning—and reverse it? Easily.

Elevate your thoughts to the spiritual level, the level of effective prayer. See the Truth: That what you desire is yours already, and is just waiting for you to be aware of it; that God wants you to have whatever you want or need. Discover also, while you are on this plane of wisdom, if you really do want this particular object, service or experience, or if another would serve you better. Once you have decided, reaffirm your awareness that all wishes have already been granted on the spiritual level, that they only await your acceptance, and give thanks in the knowledge that it will soon come to you.

The process, as I said, is easy. It is the belief that is difficult. Elevating your consciousness to the level of True Prayer is not easy. But if you follow the guidelines and repeat the prayers (as I have suggested them, or with your own improvements) you will succeed.

What we are struggling to overcome here is our subconscious conditioning. It is buried deep within us, and resists being dug out. But it is the subconscious that tells us, "The world is a hard place. Things just don't come that easily. It's all wishful thinking. I don't really believe I can have everything I want. Besides, maybe I don't deserve to have my prayers answered..." The only way to fight these deeply ingrained feelings—the product of years of experience, from birth on—is to deny them verbally, substituting the positive Truth of God's boundless love, of the perfection that is the universe, of your right as an expression of God to perfect happiness. A psychiatrist will tell you that an established belief or habit is hard to break unless a positive one is substituted in its place. It's like removing a flawed stone from a wall: The gap must be filled with a solid new stone of the proper size, or the wall will crumble. Thus, Metaphysics first denies that there is any wrong or evil, and then puts in its place the Truth of universal perfection. And the Truth, as it has been said, shall make you free.

Let's go back to childhood conditioning. Let's say your parents never said, "We can't afford it." Instead, they said, "God wants us to have this; He's just waiting for the right time to surprise us." Think about it. This thought is totally positive. It tells the spiritual Truth about God and the universe. It creates hope—and belief. And the concept of money never enters into it. It's a thought you should memorize and use whenever the lack of money intrudes into your wishes. Because this childishly simple statement is an affirmation that all comes from God, and that your fixed and prohibitive ideas about your income or economic status have no bearing on the matter. We are too caught up in the idea that, should our source of income fail, our lives would become disasters. We forget the fact that the true source of prosperity and abundance is infinite, that every need comes complete with its corresponding fulfillment on the spiritual plane—or, to put it in terms of both metaphysics and economics: Supply and demand are one and the same. On the physical plane need and fulfillment are separate and opposite; in Truth, they are inseparable because they are one.

We forget, too, that God's bounty is infinite; that he wants us to have what we want, and that this bounty will come to us at precisely the moment when it is most needed and will be most enjoyed. But you must be aware that all is available to you, or it will continue to elude you. If you have been waiting for years, feeling an intense lack of something in your life, that something has in fact been there all along, waiting for you to recognize its existence—but you had refused to open the door to it, because your subconscious had simply been following orders, turning fulfillment away because it had been conditioned to the idea that your wish was foolish, that it was financially out of reach, that it was too difficult to achieve or that you didn't deserve it.

The Bible tells us: "All the soil you stand on is yours by right of inheritance." Your feet symbolize understanding, and the soil symbolizes manifestation. Thus, any manifestation that you are able to conceive has already been granted you. In other words, what you want is already there, right at your feet. And nothing can alter this fact, because both you and everything in the universe are creations of God. Inseparable.

"He is waiting for the right moment." It is childish to expect instant gratification. There are many reasons why a wish may not be granted as soon as the words are spoken. The commonest of these is a lack of constancy, the deep and powerful belief that is necessary if your prayer is to be effective.

Doubt will render your prayer useless. Talking about your wishes before they are granted weakens prayer. Expressing concepts not consistent with spiritual Truth (a wish having revenge or a desire for domination over others, for example) will make your prayer empty and meaningless. But you must not lose patience with yourself or feel doubt because of the delay. You can't blame your subconscious for being weighed down by the accumulation of a lifetime of old ideas and habits. Look for the obstruction and remove it. You are just beginning to learn. Though the fact of your perfection is a Truth of the Spiritual plane, you have not achieved it on this earthly level.

Once your wish is expressed as perfectly as you can make it, there is no need to repeat it. You may, of course, give thanks as often as you wish—what Emmet Fox refers to as "treating a treatment." Whenever you find yourself wondering why your wish has not been granted yet, the following approach is effective:

"I have made my prayer as well as I know how. I have no need to feel worry or anxiety. I know that you have heard me and that my wish will be manifested at the proper time. I thank you Father."

When you get a surprise gift, even one you have been wishing for, it is a surprise. The above treatment's phrasing is meant to prepare you for the surprise God holds for you. This confident expectation (which may manifest itself when you least expect it!) is the faith that moves mountains—and causes wishes to be granted. Don't confuse expectation and faith with hope. "Hope," as Dr. Fox says, "is a poor relative of Faith." Hope is anxiety mixed with doubts. Faith is happy, confident expectancy. Note the difference in meaning between "I hope he'll be on time" and "I know he'll be here on time." Faith is knowing. Hope is not knowing.

When it comes to money, we must learn to think in terms of abundance, not of lack. As Professor Fillmore says, "All anxious thoughts must be banished, and we must imitate the ways of nature, and when you add to this attitude the realization that all manner of unlimited resources are at your fingertips, then the Divine Law of Prosperity will have been fulfilled."

To abandon these worries, we must meditate on abundance already manifested. We must find what old thinking or conditioning is interfering with our prosperity. And we must affirm, with all our belief, that we are the children of God and heirs to all our Father's possessions. We must know that not only does God want to see us surrounded by manifestations of wealth and happiness, but that all of mankind wishes the same for us, that no one wishes to deprive us, because all of humanity is a part of God, and God neither divides Himself nor competes with Himself, for this would result in disharmony, which is impossible in the Spiritual universe.

There is a way to produce swift results in answer to an urgent need. It will not work to produce constant abundance, but it can serve to fill the requirements of the moment.

The key lies in your powers of imagination. Picture a $50 or $100 bill in your hand. Feel its texture, its crispness. Think of the details of it, the engraving of Franklin or Grant, the rendering of the Capitol or Independence Hall, the placement of the numbers on the bill. Once you have a solid picture in your mind, proceed to imagine that you are receiving huge numbers of these bills, so many that you are at a loss as to where to put it all. Picture yourself stuffing them into your wallet, into a strongbox, making huge deposits in the bank. Imagine having enough so that you can give money away; try to feel the intense satisfaction of being able to provide for needy people, and picture the glow of happiness on their faces. You must repeat this over and over until your images are so real you can almost feel them, so that the thought impresses itself on your mind as a fact, rather than a wish, always affirming that this bounty will come to you with the blessing of God, in perfect order and harmony. Never ask where the money will come from. Do not doubt that it will come. Remember, God wants you to have it, and He is aware of your urgency. Remember, too, that the bounty might take an unexpected form, equally suited to your needs— perhaps as an extension of your indebtedness that will give you more time to come up with the money by more conventional means, the discovery that the bank has made an error (or you have) resulting in a larger bank balance than you thought, or the repayment of a loan you had forgotten or chalked off as a loss. The problem will be solved, and more important, you will have established a direct channel to God, which will remain always open.

The Tithing Habit: Giving 10% to God

*T*he concept of tithing—setting aside 10% of your income for good works—has long been a practice in many religions and of many of the followers of metaphysical Truth. So much so that these people think of their income as being only 90% of what it actually is. (We are not talking about setting aside 10% of what we manage to save, but of our total net income.) The process is automatic, a habit few would ever dream of breaking. And it isn't as painful as it sounds. The difference between living on an annual net income of $25,000 and one of $22,500 is not a major one, particularly on a paycheck-to-paycheck basis. And when your income reaches $100,000 a year—well, there are few people who can't make it on $90,000.

The true value of tithing is that it is the right thing to do. The benefit is that those who do so will never lack for money, will never experience financial problems as long as they continue the practice.

The practice is becoming more common in recent years, but the Spiritual Principle behind it is not widely known. First, tithing must be done as a voluntary act—not out of a sense of obligation or duty or any other guilt-driven motivation. Nor can it be done as an "investment"— solely for the benefits that will accrue. It must be a completely spiritual act, done for its own sake, a sharing of the wealth of Spiritual Truth.

Tithing is recommended in the Bible on numerous occasions. In Malachi 3:10:

> *Bring ye all the tithes into the storehouse, that there may be meat in mine house, and prove me now herewith, saith the Lord of Hosts, if I will not open you the windows of heaven, and pour you out a blessing that there shall not be room enough to receive it.*

Many Masters of the Truth have testified to the benefits of tithing. One of them, John Murray, wrote:

According to Hebraic Law, tithe means "the tenth part" and refers to a certain tax practice under which the Hebrew people had to contribute, according to Levitical Law, the tenth part of their produce (whether from the land or in animal form, etc.) towards God's service. It is to be noted that as long as this custom prevailed, the Hebrew nation prospered, collectively and individually, and wherever it has been applied with honesty and regularity, it has never failed. If the farmer denied the earth a certain amount of corn and potatoes of those the earth yielded up to him, there would be no harvest.

> *Why, then, do we expect to receive abundance from God, if we, in return, give so eagerly of our own goods to His holy cause? Those who tithe know they will have God as a partner.*

The link between tithing and prosperity is, after all, nothing more than an expression of the spiritual Law which tells us that whatever we do for or offer the Universe comes back to us. That which we give, whether generously or not, we shall get back in the same measure. What we plant, we shall reap: No man escapes from that Law.

*And all tithing from the Land, be it from the seeds or from
the fruit of the trees, belong to the Lord. It is blessed by
the Lord.*

LEVITICUS 27:30

*Honor the Lord with thy substance, and with the first
fruits of all thine increase. So shall thy barns be filled
with plenty, and thy presses burst out with new wine.*

PROVERBS 3:9-10

After Jacob saw the vision, which explained that there was
a mystical ladder from Earth to Heaven (the symbolic ladder,
representing our communicative link to God through Scientific Prayer
and ethical behavior), he immediately vowed to adopt the practice of
tithing, knowing that:

*God will be with me and will protect me in my journey
through life; He will provide me with bread and clothing.*

The logical question remains: How to disburse these funds in
God's work? First, it is necessary to set this money aside, totally
separate from your own savings. I recommend a separate savings
account (there's no reason why God's money shouldn't earn interest),
which should be treated as a custodial account, since that's precisely
what it is—money which is not yours, but over which you have the
responsibility to see that it is spent in the proper manner.

As to how this money is spent, I must leave that to you. My personal
feeling is that it is best spent in spreading Metaphysical Truth, which
is why I have spent most of my tithings on free lectures (from which
this series of books is derived). My reasoning is that propagating this
knowledge and supporting the institutions and activities dedicated

to expanding metaphysical awareness is the most effective way of benefiting mankind as a whole. For every human being who studies the Truth and learns to use it in the betterment of his own life and that of his fellows represents a small betterment in the Spiritual health of mankind. Most students of spiritual principles agree. However, you may feel that specific charities or even assistance to the needy on an individual basis is just as valuable. Simply keep in mind that God wants only the best for all his children, and for you to be His assistant in helping to make it possible. As long as these funds are spent or donated in the true spirit of selflessness and dedicated to building spiritual harmony, they will be well spent.

One final word: You are under no obligation to tithe; in fact, you should not begin to do so until your heart and conscience tell you the time is right, and you can do so in joy and without regret. (This has nothing to do with your financial position at the moment. A person might feel that finances are too tight right now, that they'll start tithing when things get better. That person is missing the point. It is when things are difficult that tithing is most valuable. Remember that worries on the physical plane are due to mental conditioning, and that Scientific Prayer and spiritual acts can only alter this conditioning. The sacrifice of tithing is one such spiritual act—but it must be done freely and in the spirit of goodwill, not as a selfish "investment." If material thoughts are your motivation, it cannot, by definition, be a spiritual act, and it will be a total failure.)

Remember also that tithing is not a sometime thing. Once entered into, it must be continued, with every paycheck, dividend check or windfall, without fail. You can't just set that 10% aside when the money's flowing in and let it slide when times get tough. (After all, when very little money is coming in, then it'll only be 10% of very little.)

Tithing is an act of Faith. And for the truly faithful, its rewards are many.

Where Are You Now?

*I*f you find that you're comfortable with everything you've read thus far; if you find yourself thinking, "I knew this instinctively, without being told," or, "I must be a born metaphysician, because I've been practicing many of these principles all my life,"—then you have been through many of the sects, religions and philosophies that have existed on this planet through your other past lives. You have accumulated their practices and theories, and past experience has shown you which of these are valid and which are to be discarded. The constructive, valid ideas remain a part of your Causal Body, of the Aura of your Higher Self (the spiritual "I"). The erroneous or destructive parts, if not discarded, may manifest themselves in your "inferior vehicles"— physical appearance, emotional structure, etheric body and mental frame. Your etheric (spiritual) body houses all the memories of everything that has ever happened to you in all your previous lives. Nothing is ever lost. This is most important: Nothing is ever lost.

If you feel akin to the metaphysical teachings, if you understand them easily and find yourself immersed in them, it means that you are prepared to take the next step up. If you do not accept them, if you find them difficult to understand, if you consider them foolish, unpleasant or feel an aversion to them, it only means that you are not yet ready to "digest" them. For now, you'd do best to continue following the religion you are comfortable with, where the Principle of Mentalism is not practiced. Your chosen beliefs will serve you well, offering you knowledge and comfort in your everyday life. They will also entail various rites, rituals, physical practices and restrictions, diets and denials—all of which can be summed up in one word: Limitations. But if you feel you need these beliefs, then this is your present stage, and you should remain with it as long as you remain comfortable. If you continue to study the principles of metaphysics, you will begin to feel these limitations and gravitate toward metaphysical beliefs.

Be assured that this is in no way a criticism of you or of any doctrine. It is merely a statement of your stage of development, a stage everyone must go through on the road to Spiritual Truth. Few people are ready to move on in just a few weeks or months of study. My only desire is to make this spiritual progress as easy and comfortable as possible.

Metaphysics is a system not only of Principles but also of action. It is a doctrine given to us by those whom we call Masters of Wisdom (Christ was one such master.) It is both spiritual and eminently practical. It is designed to make life a daily celebration of joy and harmony— rather than a day-to-day struggle for survival. No other doctrine shows you how to give yourself your "heart's desire" by expressing your wishes (Getting Started), or shows you how to solve your problems (Master Key). No other tells you how to guide your business dealings smoothly and harmoniously to ultimate success (God and Business), how to realize material benefits in a short time (money, Tithing) or how to produce immediate spiritual development (The Presence, A Verbal Approach to Developing Divine Love.) The principles of metaphysics are not simply laws to be obeyed, in the hope of better life in the hereafter; they are tools to be used, for a better life in the here and now.

This here and now, we call the New Era, and it is an era of freedom. A period during which we have seen and will see the gradual disappearance of all the complicated rites, the countless details of outworn custom that take so much time away from the important pursuits of life. In the past, notably during the period of the Temple of Jerusalem, Judaism taught that everyone had to observe more than six hundred different ritualistic details in the course of a single day. The poor lived under a consciousness of ineptitude (for who could actually fulfill such a daily obligation?), of slavery, of sin; they were punished, and punished themselves, mercilessly for being unable to follow the letter of such rigid laws. (The Creative Principle of Law of Mentalism teaches that to believe oneself to be a sinner is to create such a state.)

Though I do not wish to denigrate any religion, I feel it necessary to say that if your religion's doctrine or its leaders preach that illness, misery, poverty and tragedy are punishments from God, or are to be suffered as the burden of sin, then that religion teaches error (which incidentally, is the true meaning of the word "sin.") I would advise you to turn a deaf ear to such teachings: You have evolved beyond them.

Later on in your metaphysical studies, you will learn to "burn" your karma, or that of another. (By applying the cleansing Divine Violet Flame of Freedom through Love. This was a gift left by the Ascended Master, Count Saint-Germain, a prophet of the New Era.) By that time, you will be able to invoke from within your own Causal Body all the knowledge and abilities you have accumulated through previous lives. But for now, you may begin practicing this formula:

"I AM the Divine Wisdom of God. He knows
everything in me…"

And continue with the affirmation in the chapter "The Power of Verbalization." (Page 103).

The Practice of God's Presence (as these studies are called) will begin a cleansing process within you, and will free you from past errors. It is a process that teaches almost without the need of books. (As Jesus said, "The Holy Spirit, which my Father will send you in my name, will teach you all things.") It will begin to free you from the multitude of constraints and limitations which you once thought were necessary duties, and one of the greatest freedoms you will achieve will be to learn to solve someone else's problems from afar, even to cure from a distance, for you yourself will no longer suffer from such problems and ailments. This will free you to perform you work in the physical plane without archaic limitations. There will even be times when your mere presence (as the expression of Spiritual and Divine Consciousness) will turn situations around; this consciousness will produce "sympathetic vibrations" in those around you, elevating them to a higher spiritual level. This consciousness, shown in you and in others, is, in fact, THE consciousness, THE very presence of God!

Who and What is Christ?

*P*eople familiar with the New Testament know of Christ as an individual, a prophet, the Son of God on earth. But they speak only on His physical manifestation. On the metaphysical level, He is not so much being as an essence. In My lectures, I speak of Christ as our Truth—The perfect and all-powerful Truth that is the best and noblest part of us.

Let's get back to basics and work up. Let's start with Life. Life is anything that hears, feels or responds. If it is earthly life, it can be animal, vegetable or even mineral. If it is basic or spiritual life, it can be air, fire or water.

All life has individuality. Though all life is one, each fragment shows its own special and distinctive talents or attributes, very much like the specialized cells that make up your body.

A man may have skin that is white, black or any shade in between; his eyes may be blue or brown or any number of variations of the two. He may be a pygmy, a giant, a mathematician, an artist, outspoken or quit, beautiful or ugly. There are infinite varieties between races, virtues, peculiarities, talents, dimensions and capabilities. Why, then, do we say that all humankind is one—that all Life is one?

Simply because all—absolutely all that is—comes from only one source, which is God. All living things are children of God; and, while each as unique, each shares this common origin.

There is infinite individuality, and there is sameness. Just as there is resemblance in the members of a family, of a race, of the species homo sapiens in general. The same is true on the spiritual level. There are those non-physical aspects which mark us as relatives of God. They are Consciousness, Intelligence and Love. All living things possess these attributes in some degree. And these attributes have their auras in the spiritual spectrum. Consciousness, the awareness of life, or will, is represented by Blue. Intelligence or reasoning is represented by Yellow, and the attractions, repulsions and attachments of Love represented by Red. These are the Primary Colors, from which all other colors are derived, just as the attributes they represent are those from which all other characteristics stem.

We have said that all Life hears, feels and responds. But human ears are deficient. The most receptive ear cannot hear tones outside the range of 15 cycles to 25,000 cycles per second—much less hear a plant cry out or the motion of the cells in his own body. It is a limitation of the physical plane. But on the higher etheric and astral planes, there are infinite voices to be heard—the voices of all the things that have life. It would be too much for the human mind and body to bear alone, without the presence of Christ to filter, translate, soften and clarify what would only be a thunderous cacophony without Him. And when the spiritual senses awake in you, you will need His presence, His love and solace.

We know as much as we can of who Christ was from the Bible. What He was, and is, is a more complex subject. He is the ultimate outward expression of the three attributes of Life: Consciousness, Intelligence and Love, in their highest essences. He is Consciousness of the most intense Blue, the will of God Himself; He is the shining Golden intelligence that is God's omniscience; and He is the highest and most all-encompassing Love, the deepest, purest of Reds. He is everything we are in its purest distillation, the highest level on a scale of perfection. He is the pattern and design of God's will for all of us.

Our daily meditations should include thinking about the metaphysical Christ: His manifestation as the divine attributes of Man. Spend but a minute thinking about Him in each of these attributes. About the purest meaning of Consciousness and divine will. You will experience something like the sensation of taking a step upward. Think of Intelligence, of the all-knowingness of God as expressed in Christ, and in us. Think of pure Love, infinite in capacity, endless in duration. These are our links with God, the "family resemblances" that bring us closer to Him through Christ as our brother, and as God's purest expression of what humanity can aspire to.

If we do this every day, we shall come to resemble His design for perfection more and more. We shall become more alert and alive, more intelligent, more capable of love. For Christ is all that God meant Life to be; he hears us and responds in perfection.

Remember that in these books, the metaphysical "Christ" of which we speak is not only the Jesus of this era's New Testament, but the idea of a perfect being who is God's closest representative, and an essence which is God's closest representation. There is a cosmic Christ, an individual Christ—that is a Divine being, created by God, who has developed like a seed through the 14,000 years of the evolution of man as a conceptual thinker. This Christ is an intelligent being, alive in each one of us, caring about each of us more than we ourselves do. He has given us breath and sustained us throughout our evolution, and only waits for the opportunity to demonstrate the purpose of the divine project which each of us is. If you begin to accept this fact, you will let God, through you, continue to fulfill His own pattern of perfection. As a beginning, pause here. Place your hand on your heart, so that you can feel the pulse of Life, and make this affirmation:

I now accept the Truth that I possess within me a Divine Being, which is at this very moment developing and bringing to my life and my senses the realization of my own divinity. I affirm that in my mind there is a Point of Power called Faith, a source of strength which guarantees that I will never lack for Faith. I know that I have God within me, that all my being is composed of God Himself, and therefore that I have all the qualities and attributes of God Himself. Thank you Lord, for granting me this strength and this Truth.

It is said that each cosmic cycle (about 2,000 years) is marked by the appearance of a Perfect Being, a "Christ," who dwells among us and brings to humanity a body of wisdom or philosophy appropriate to the times, usually expressed as a religion. There is much of values in each of these bodies of belief, and that which remains is incorporated into other major religions; this is why the religions of India still have influence on contemporary thought, why there is so much of Judaism Christianity and Islam, why Metaphysics draws on the strengths of all religions in the effort to bring mankind closer to God's perfection.

We are rapidly approaching to the end of one such cycle. Our planet is threatened by chaos, even by physical destruction because humankind resists change, and so many are blind to the Truth that lies before them. We are now in a period of rapid transition, of evolution. The New Era of Metaphysics is around the corner. There may be a new Perfect Being, a new "Christ" among us even now—but we must remember that He is not always recognized for what He is: It is up to us to seek the wisdom of this New Era through our individual consciousness and the elevation of that consciousness to the Spiritual plane.

Life

*O*ne of the aspects of the Creator is Life itself. God is Life: Your Life and mine, and the Life of everything that exists.

Life is only one. That of human beings, of plants and insects, birds and bacteria—of everything that moves or reacts. Life does not belong to us individually; it is a quality we share. We are, each of us, merely molecules in the ocean of Life.

This is contrary to what we are used to thinking; we view ourselves as having a certain quantity of life measured out to us; we believe that, like a small puddle in the sun, it begins evaporating as soon as it is formed, and may be obliterated or polluted by a fateful shovelful of dirt. But, in truth, nothing can touch or contaminate the ever-flowing spring that feeds the infinite ocean of life—for that spring is God. Life itself cannot die; it exists as the antithesis of death. It is a powerful current of energy that penetrates and flows through us; we live because we are within Life.

We are brought up believing that each of us is an isolated "puddle" of life, susceptible to illnesses, accidents, ageing and death, and we live by these thoughts and pass them on to our children and others. We must substitute positive spiritual Truth for these negative notions. The more each of us meditates on the Truth of Perfection, the more we deny the negative and affirm the positive, the more we pass on this knowledge—the more of us will be elevated to the level of spiritual Truth, and sooner humanity will be free of the physical limitations our beliefs have saddled us with.

Jesus said, "The Kingdom of Heaven is like yeast taken by a woman and hidden in three measures of flour, until all was leavened." In other words, the small number of us who have experienced spiritual Truth will pass along that Truth until all mankind is "leavened," and all people will know the perfect state of happiness, harmony and growth on the physical level that has always existed on the spiritual plane. Pain and illness, ageing and death will no longer be necessary.

To most people, this sounds too miraculous to be believed. But what is a miracle but that which is beyond our ordinary experience? It was not so long ago that a man with a lighter, creating flame from nothing with a flick of his thumb, or a gun, which delivered thunderous invisible death from afar, would be considered a god by natives in remote parts of the world—because these abilities, so commonplace to us, were totally beyond their experience. Thus the true state of things on the spiritual plane appears miraculous to the majority who are totally immersed in the physical world.

But there are miracles even in everyday life—miracles that are so familiar to us that we take them for granted. Isn't the creation of a third life from the union of a miracle? And what about the everyday conversion of energy into matter: The growth of a tree from a tiny seed, the process of photosynthesis that converts pure sunlight into food?

As human beings, we are somewhat miraculous ourselves. We combine the earthly, physical aspects of the animal kingdom (eating, drinking, reproducing) with those divine aspects of the higher planes (thinking, love, creativity). We take all this for granted. Yet some find it difficult to believe one of the basic Truths of metaphysics: That evolution is a continuing process, and that in the millennia to come, humanity will gradually sever its ties with the animal kingdom, and physical pain, illness, ageing, even the need to eat and drink will no longer be necessary.

It may be that some people have attained that spiritual level in our own time. There is the well-documented case of Teresa Neumann, a woman in Germany who manifested the stigmata of open wounds in her hands and feet every good Friday. What is considerably more astonishing is the fact that these wounds became permanent, always open, though they never became infected or bled copiously—and then Teresa Neumann simply stopped taking any form of food or drink. The German Government assigned full-time investigators to the case, watching over her 24 hours a day. Over a period during which any human being would have died of thirst and starvation many times over, she was never seen to touch a morsel or so much as a drop of water, and the authorities testified to this. She lived another 45 healthy years—and during this time, no one, even those relatives, friends and loved ones nearest her, ever saw her take nourishment in any physical form!

In the metaphysical light, we see that, in the Bible, the words "eat" and "drink" are often used to mean "meditate" and "think." Drink and thought are both considered liquid in nature—easily swallowed. Food and meditation, however, require "chewing" in both the physical and mental sense—taking longer to prepare for digestion. Thus, when Jesus said, "He who eats of my flesh and drinks of my blood has eternal life," He was telling us to think and meditate on the lessons He had taught—to partake of the Truth.

Meditate, then, about Life as it is expressed spiritually: That vast ocean of which we are part of. Life that simply is, needing no sustenance other than the Creator from which it springs.

Death

*W*hen a small child dies, or when a young mother or father passes away, leaving children and family bereft—when anyone dies "before his time," there is always someone who'll be on hand to say something like, "This is God's way of testing you; we must all bow before God's will." Students of the Truth find such thoughts downright blasphemous. Do we not know that God wishes nothing but good for His children? He does not use pain and misery to "test" us at His whim. Such a God would be a cruel one, driving us to a faith in evil rather than perfection—and such are the Gods invented by so many of mankind's creeds.

First of all, we know that death does not truly exist, that it is no more than a change in lifestyles, one of the many transitions a person makes in his or her own personal evolution.

As a family grows and the house they live in becomes too small for their needs, they move to a larger, better home; when clothing is outgrown or becomes threadbare, it is discarded. Houses and clothing and countless other things in life outlive their usefulness. This is all death is: Casting aside a physical framework that is no longer appropriate. Thus the aphorism, "Only the good die young" takes on a new and more meaningful significance—for only the good, the spiritually enlightened, are ready to "shuffle off this mortal coil" before "their time." God's will is that all human beings fulfill their missions and come to the end of their earthly lives with the full use of their faculties, strong and well. It is neither to God's advantage nor to the individual's to waste part of one's stay on earth deaf, half blind,

helplessly senile. But God will not cut short a lifetime whose purpose
has not been fulfilled either.

When a very old person dies, no one really feels a deep despair
over it. Such a death usually leaves us with a loving feeling, good
memories—a sense of completion, rather than one of loss. People
around the deceased return to their interests, their families without
any major disruption. Someone will often say, "Life goes on." How
true! Life does go on; and that infinite, timeless ocean called Life still
contains the essence of the "deceased."

This is God's will: That people accept the passing of a loved one
with a minimum sorrow, with pleasant memories and the awareness
that this was only a passage to a better life.

Thus, death is not to be feared, however early or late in a person's
life it may come. It is such fears—not God's will—that may contribute
to the shortening of a loved one's effective stay on Earth. The energy
of fear would be far better expended in a prayer: "I have faith that
all of my loved ones will live long and happy lives, and fulfill their
purpose in this life, according to God's plan. Thank you Father, for
I know you have heard me." And whenever negative thoughts, such
as fearing for the death of one dear to you, push them aside with the
affirmation: "There is no reason for fear; I do not need it: I know the
Truth."

This faith, this knowledge of the Truth, can create positive
vibrations all around it. The presence of a Master, one who has
experienced great spiritual enlightenment, can actually cause a cure.
Positive "vibrations" cancel out the negative; light always obliterates
darkness; Truth destroys a lie. A Master metaphysician will remember
Christ's words—"I have been granted total dominion over Heaven and
Earth"—and will apply his Faith, the power of the Christ within him,
to the Faith of the sick one, and will declare the Truth of the patient's
cure.

It's natural to ask, "What if the person has an incurable illness? What if he or she has been in a major accident that has destroyed a vital organ? What if the person does not survive no matter what is done?"

First, we must remember that nothing is impossible to God. This is a statement to be taken literally. If a person has fulfilled God's plan for him, then he will pass on to the next level of existence—and a Master will know this, and not attempt to intervene. In the case of the loss of a vital organ, or incurable illness, we should be aware that all measures are of God—including organ transplants and remissions.

And, as we know, Life itself is indestructible, and when Faith is present, it will repair itself, even on the physical plane, unless human minds obstruct the process with doubt and erroneous beliefs.

Remember, too, that God does not interfere with free will. If the patient doubts that a cure is possible, or no longer even wishes to be cured, there is nothing any human agency can do about it. Life will go on, but it will go on to another plane of existence.

In performing His healing miracles, Jesus would often say, "Your Faith has saved you." In mankind the blind see, the crippled walk, even in bringing Lazarus back from death, He proved that Faith does not accept the "impossible."

And when a disciple would ask, "Why, when I did everything as you told me, was I not able to do what you can do?" Jesus would answer simply, "Your Faith was not great enough." He would not chide his followers for a lack of Faith, for He knew that Faith came only with knowledge. Instead, he would tell them: "All these things I do, you will also do, and greater things as well." He did not claim special abilities as the Son of God; rather he called Himself the "Son of Man." He told them: "You are of God," adding, "Verily I say unto you that if you had faith the size of a grain of mustard, you could bid this mountain move from here to there, and it would happen."

Jesus taught metaphysics. And all who study this Truth will be able to perform the miracles he promised his disciples.

As you've probably noticed, sometimes "miracles" happen to people who have never heard the word metaphysics. The reason for this is simple: Some people have the "Faith that moves mountains" without having to study about it. You may think of it as instinctive, but, more likely, it's the subconscious awareness of what they've learned in past lives. Or perhaps it comes as the result of a good upbringing or religious background. But the key is Faith, the ability to place one's thoughts in God, in Christ, or simply in the spiritual plane; this is trust, a relaxation of anxiety that allows one to sit back in confident expectation.

People have complained to me that they did everything they were told, to no avail. All I have to do is reach out and touch such a person's trapezius—the muscle that runs between the neck and the shoulder— and feel the rock hardness of the tension there to give him his answer. Faith relaxes; hope, which is partly doubt, creates tension.

Another cause of this failure is telling others about the cure you will provoke (or the wish that's about to come true for you). As I have said, this greatly weakens the effects of your prayers and meditations. Such talk is not spreading the Truth, but a kind of bragging, and is born of pride, not of Faith. When Jesus cured the sick, he would often say, "Go in peace, and tell no one of this." It was not so much matter of humility as it was part of the "treatment," a preservation of the power of Faith. Words are spoken thoughts; they are atmospheric vibrations, a dispersal of energy, and therefore a diminution of the strength of your efforts. Do not speak of your accomplishments until long after the fact, and then with humility add an explanation that such accomplishments are God's work, that the only power is that of prayer and Faith.

Psychologists and psychiatrists have discovered in this century what metaphysicians have always known: The direct relationship between how a person thinks and how a person feels. Even general medicine, generally skeptical about recognizing mental and spiritual effects, has finally acknowledged the role of stress in ulcers, cardiac conditions and even cancer.

All repressed feelings, emotions not given an outlet for fear of sinning or offending, or for reasons of guilt, will find another physical outlet, expressed in everything from a mere malaise to asthma to hysteria, blindness and paralysis.

There are even feelings which are too intense for the human body contain, what we refer to as the "abstract negative." Such collective negatives as prejudice, a reasonless, consuming hatred against another race or religion; hatred or fear between nations. Often the pressure is relieved through war—with terrible destruction on both sides—or through oppression, famine, plague and even "natural" disasters.

There are also those "abstract positives," so high, so spiritual and beautiful that the human body is too crudely wrought to contain them. These are expressed in music, poetry, painting, sculpture, architecture—spilling over into the natural wonders which surround us, and sometimes are even expressed in partly abstract, partly idealized human forms, which we call "angels." (Angels are powerful and positive entities, created by the ideals of man out of the divine material of affirmative spiritual feeling.)

The power of feelings expresses itself in every aspect of life. It is said that mother's prayers go straight to the ear of God—and this is more than poetic hyperbole, for when a mother's love is as pure and selfless as we imagine it to be, it projects protective angelic forms toward the child. But when that love is tainted with fear and anxiety, its expression is no longer angelic, but negative, bringing about the realization of those fears. The child may be sickly, accident-prone, may even die prematurely. And the grieving mother, knowing no better, is either bitter or believes it to be God's will and suffers in resignation.

Such tragedy is so unnecessary. It represents neither the Truth nor God's will. And it is easily warded off. When fears and anxieties threaten to distort love, the metaphysical treatment is simply to say: "According to God's will, I do not want any of my loved ones to suffer illness, accidents or to die before having fulfilled their purpose and full term on earth; therefore there will be no need for suffering: I shall not suffer from their departure, nor shall they suffer because of mine. This is God's law, and I embrace it wholeheartedly. Thank you Father for hearing me, and for your Love." (If you feel ready to include people other than those in your immediate family in your loving thoughts, so much the better.)

You never need to fear the pain of death; yours or any loved ones. Generally, people reject thoughts of death with horror or angry protestations. This is counter-productive, since it adds other negative emotions to a negative thought. Instead, it is best to treat it with calm, firm denial: "The thought of death has no place in my life. I do not need it. It is gone, because I know the Truth, and the Truth is Life." Then go on to thinking of other things.

Spontaneous and intrusive thoughts of death are generally bit your own; they are usually the thoughts of others, so pervasive because death is such a prominent fear with so many. (We are, after all, the only animal that contemplates the possibility of its own death.) When Jesus said, "The last enemy to conquer is Death," he referred to the fear of death as well. For it is that very fear—that stress—than contributes to a person's dying before his time.

Senility, too, is a physical ill that we need not fear of suffer. As long as we stay on earth, there is no reason that we should not do so in full possession of our senses, faculties and mobility. Again, when any debilitating condition begins to manifest itself—failing eyesight, hearing or memory, stiffening joints and so forth—remember that this not as it should be, not as it is in the perfection of the spiritual plane. ("As it is above, so it is below.") You must make an affirmation, firmly, and without anger or fear: "No—I will not accept this because it is not God's will. Infirmity is an absurd idea, and I have no use for it. It can not be because I know the Truth, and the Truth is Health."

And never forget that the Truth includes physical treatments as well. Man was given the ability to develop medical knowledge, and that knowledge is not to be ignored. If there is a diet, an exercise program, a medical remedy available to you, make use of it. The developments of man in healing and bettering himself came about through God's gift of intelligence and awareness, and God's gift—whether they take the form of aspirin or the ability to pray effectively—are not to be ignored. Such positive remedies as vaccines are "angels": Creations of both man and God.

"Angels" are useful visualizations when we wish to protect others and ourselves from harm and unhappiness. When you go to sleep, place an angel at every door and window. You will be leaving potent vibrations of good surrounding your home, and bad intentions cannot penetrate. (Darkness cannot exist in the presence of light, for it is no more that the absence of light.) Whenever loved ones travel, visualize an angel next to the driver (or pilot, or captain). They will be protected, through your faith. These abstract beings are your will and God's combined. It is a powerful combination.

And remember, it is the fear of death that brings death before its time. And the death that comes to us when our mission on earth is fulfilled is not an end to life, but a transition to life of another kind. It is rebirth, continuation. In Truth, death does not exist at all. There is only Life. And there is only one Presence in your life, one power. Only the Presence of omnipotent good which we call God.

Metaphysics and Medicine

*F*or the purposes of this chapter, we'll be speaking of medicine as though it had only two major branches: General and specialized, i.e., those disciplines with treat the whole body, such as Family medicine (or General Practice), and those which treat only specific areas or problems, such as ENT, Cardiology, Osteopathy, Psychiatry and so on.

The generalists and most specialists—other than psychiatrists—share one trait in common: They assume that whatever illness the patient manifests is physical in origin (although some Family Practitioners adopt a more holistic approach, particularly those who know their patients as neighbors and friends—a rare situation these days).

Psychiatrists, on the other hand, though they will investigate the possibility of physical origins for their patients' problems (particularly in the area of neurological disorders and chemical imbalances), are well aware that the human mind can and does produce manifestations of virtually every medical problem imaginable.

The problem is, few people go to a psychiatrist for pains in the stomach or heart. And the average physician will simply determine the nature and location the pain, diagnose the ulcer, the colitis, the angina, and prescribe a purely physical remedy for it, from Maalox to a heart bypass. Questions about stress, such as financial worries, business pressure, disharmonies in the family rarely arise, and these stresses, even when brought out, are dismissed as aggravating the condition, rather than causing it.

Students of metaphysics are aware that physical problems are created by the patient's reactions to the environment and the problems and stresses it causes in his life, and go so far as to state that almost every medical problem has psychosomatic basis. (Of course the broken bones suffered in accidents are not directly stress related—but the metaphysician goes to the roots: What caused the accident? The victim's feeling that he should be punished for some transgression? Those bones will heal faster when the guilt is treated along with the injury!)

Metaphysics, in dealing with physical illness as a symptom of a spiritual lack or disfunction, may be compared with a school of general medicine called allopathy. The allopathy physician is concerned with illness on a symptomatic level, and treats the patient by methods that will produce symptoms opposite to those of the illness. (Bringing down a dangerously high fever with an ice bath is an allopathic approach.) We work on the spiritual problem in the same way—by reversing the thinking that produces the symptoms of physical illness.

Let's start with a simplification. Happy people are rarely, if ever, ill. And when an ailment hits them, they will get over it faster, or experience a lighter case than most people. We've all noticed this. It is a clear example of mind over matter. (In more ways than one: The mental level is higher than the physical, in metaphysical thinking. We think of those aspects of ourselves as divided into bodies, with the inferior or lower bodies, in ascending order, being the physical, the mental, the etheric and the emotional. Above these are the spiritual, creative and astral planes.)

Smiling, in other words, really is good medicine. Even working strictly within the limitations of the physical plane, smiling works backwards from the lips to the brain. The set of muscles used to produce a smile are working in a way associated with happiness, contentment and well-being. The association produces other physical responses that go along with a happy state: Muscle relaxation, a sense of calmness.

And your own smile produces similar responses in others: You are, in fact, changing a stressful environment into a relaxed one with a simple change of expression.

The fact of the matter is that forming you face into a smiling expression—especially when you least feel like it—will very quickly give you a good reason for smiling!

Think how much stronger these effects are when we enter the spiritual level! For example, when you are feeling extremely sad, pressured or distraught, declare immediately, "I bless and give thanks for the good in this situation." Elevate yourself to the spiritual level and meditate on that statement. You know that God intends only good for us. Therefore it must be the good in any situation that is God's doing. All else is a distortion brought about by our own confusions and attitudes and the ambient thoughts of others. When you bless the good in a situation, you increase the power of that good. You will immediately feel better; that situation will begin to correct itself; the good will grow and overcome the bad in the situation until the problem has been neutralized, or even turned to your benefit.

The same approach is effective when you experience illness. Intestinal disorders, for example, are especially susceptible to both your smiles and your prayers, since such ailments are so directly related to the influence of nervous tension.

I cannot emphasize too strongly or too often the importance of a totally positive "treatment." If you mix thoughts or feelings of doubt or pessimism with your attempts at prayer, your efforts are negated and the result is nil. The proper approach is to begin with, "I bless and am grateful for the general good health I now enjoy." Then proceed to meditate on this. If you have an illness confined to a specific area, think about the healthy areas that surround it; if you have colitis, meditate on your healthy stomach, the strength of your abdominal muscles and so forth. Let the surrounding good squeeze out the bad on the spiritual plane. And follow your doctor's advice. He is not only helping you on the physical level but on the spiritual level as well, for he is another force who wishes you only the best of health.

The etheric body is the depository of all our memories from our past lives. Deep impressions made in those previous lives will influence and color our thinking and actions in the present life. (I know a lady who spent many previous lives as a devout Catholic, and at least one during the Victorian era, a time of repression and melodrama, when all things religious were seen as occasions of pain and suffering. As a result, she is today a repressed person, given to turning the slightest situation into a melodrama. She sees Christ as figure of pain, not of joy and love. She wishes to be a happy, but her etheric memories and her disproportionately large emotional body push her toward misery, with the result that she is only happy when she feels miserable. She will have great difficulty in accepting the metaphysical process, which strives for total happiness by aligning the four bodies into a single cooperative entity that functions in complete order and harmony.)

I'll give you an excellent example of the power of metaphysical "medicine" on a third party. Some years ago, I hired a young girl as a maid. Her previous job was one of utter stress, working for a matriarchal tyrant for whom she could do nothing right. When she came to me, she had a history of attacks of lower abdominal pain and vomiting; her doctor had diagnosed the problem as chronic appendicitis, and had told her that an operation was inevitable. To test the situation one day, I gave her three mint tablets and told her to put one in her mouth immediately, and take the other two at half-hour intervals. In less than and hour and a half, her pains had vanished. I told her that she would not have the pain again, and if it did come back, I had made an agreement with her previous employer to send her back to that job. (The unreasonable whims of employers in those days were taken for granted, and work was hard to come by.) I also told her that there was no need for her problems to come back, since it wasn't really appendicitis but a nervous condition brought about by her unhappiness in her previous job. Then I asked her if she was happy working for me (yes), if she felt comfortable in my home (yes), and if she had everything she wanted (yes). Finally I told her that she would have no such stresses in her new job, and that her pains would not come back. And for as long as she worked for me, they never did.

The Never-ending Prayer

*I*f you feel you have no time for prayer, meditation or treatments—no time for God—it is probably because you spend all your time worrying about illnesses or problems. But the fact is, whatever time you devote to spiritual matters will free you from all those worries. In the long run, a few minutes on the spiritual level will bring you hours of peace—hours you can spend on pursuits considerably more productive than weeping, wailing and gnashing of teeth.

St. Paul, in his first epistle to the Thessalonians, advised his brethren to pray constantly. Of course, he did not mean that we should spend every waking hour on our knees, in unending supplication. He meant, rather, that we should live in a prayerful state, to keep our minds and souls vibrating in a positive, higher plane. A smile is a prayer. An act of kindness is a prayer. Expressions of love, of thanks, of praise are prayers. Remaining happy, calm and at peace is a state of prayer.

Paul's own words say succinctly: "Rejoice evermore. Pray without ceasing. In every thing give thanks: For this is the will of God in Christ Jesus concerning you." He expressed in very few words the principle behind scientific prayer, the metaphysical science of life in capsule form: Be happy always and give thanks to God for everything, and you will find yourself in that state of constant prayer.

There are a few easy and practical habits that will help you maintain the state of "constant prayer." The first is simply your method of greeting people—your salutation. The word is derived from the Latin salutare, meaning to wish good health, to greet—and the secret is to take the meaning literally. In other words, whenever you say "hello" or "hi" to someone, whatever your form of greeting—put a genuine wish for that person's good health behind your words, however casual those words may be. Silently say, "I wish you the best of health" (however you wish to phrase it). And don't be stingy with your good wishes; they cost you nothing. Don't limit them to people you love, people you know or even people you like. Include every waitress, cab driver, casual acquaintance or anyone you are meeting for the first time in your wish. Make it automatic. Wish good health on your worst enemy. Wish it as you drop change in a beggar's palm. (Your wish is far more valuable than nickels and dimes, even if the recipient doesn't know it.) When you must greet someone crude, vulgar or obviously malevolent, bless the good—the "inner Christ," if you prefer—in that person. Even these, even your enemies, are of divine substance, however misdirected.

What you will be creating is an aura of good will. To most people, a greeting is a meaningless acknowledgement, no more communicative of beneficial or sincere than a grunt. But others will soon notice, consciously or otherwise, that your "hello" has real substance. People will begin greeting you with more feeling. They will be attracted to you, feel comfortable in your company. They'll pay more attention to what you say and seek your advice, in both business and social matters.

To give good health in greeting is an act of universal love. It is more than simple wish of physical well-being; it is addressed to an individual's spiritual health, a wish of light to the mind and soul -- not just the individual's, but that "oversoul," the ocean of life, of which that person is a part. An in this sense, it is a blessing directed to the universe, an effort at cleansing the universe of error and confusion by wishing for the health—the perfection—of all. And such wishes always rebound, to your benefit. "What goes around, comes around."

The second form of constant prayer lies in your approach to everything you do in daily life. That's not as tall an order as it sounds. Every day, there are things to be done, from brushing your teeth to reading the newspaper; from balancing the checkbook to dealing with a client or customer, employer or employee; from cooking to going to a party. Some activities are chores, some are pleasures. The approach is simply this: Before undertaking anything, merely say, "I dedicate this to the Good." If you've forgotten and you're in the middle of a business meeting or changing the sparkplugs, say it then. The important thing is to dedicate the activity. Chores will become lighter, less wearisome. Pleasant events will become more so. (And not only for you! Other people involved in their daily activities will find their own burdens a little lighter, their own pleasures a little greater: Such is the strength of the waves of goodwill you will be projecting!) Your every activity will have become a highly effective prayer.

The third form is to let your last activity of the day be a prayer. Whether you are accustomed to saying prayers at bedtime or not, let your last thoughts before retiring be: "I forgive all who need forgiveness from me, and I forgive myself as well for any wrong or error I may have committed. I extend this forgiveness to the spiritual plane, even though forgiveness is unnecessary there, because I wish my good will to exist on the spiritual level, to counteract any ill will that may be directed against me. I invite my spiritual guides to use my sleeping hours to compose my mind and guide me to do good wherever it is needed. Thank you Father for hearing me." This prayer not only provides the benefits you request, but brings a serenity that makes falling into a sound, healthful sleep as easy as closing your eyes.

As you can see, "praying constantly" takes almost no time at all, yet it affects every moment of your day. Everyone you meet, everything you do is enhanced by your good wishes, your dedications and your forgiveness, and you will have created about yourself a spiritual aura that radiates goodwill, and draws the good wishes of others toward you. Making the three approaches above a part of your daily pattern will keep you in constant touch with the spiritual plane—in touch with God. And when you are in touch with God, there will be no need to worry about illnesses and other problems.

About Spiritism

As you delve deeper into the study of metaphysics, you'll find that few of your fellow students are also followers of spiritism. It is not so much that the two areas are incompatible; it is simply a matter of differing goals.

It may well be that you or some of your fellow students were spiritists, perhaps even mediums or clairvoyants, in one or more past lives. But few people will remember those lives, and fewer still will carry over the traits and talents acquired in a previous existence (though there is often subconscious influence on the etheric level). The reason these abilities are not carried over is usually that the need for them does not exist in this life. We are in a state of personal evolution, casting aside the unnecessary, developing new skills with every incarnation. Psychic abilities exact a considerable toll from those who have them. Those who are sensitive to the spirit world (as distinct from the spiritual) are subject to many distracting influences; the disembodied, having nothing better to do, often plague the sensitive with pranks and torments that can become terrifying. The study of metaphysics requires concentration, an environment of peace and harmony—quite the opposite of the turmoil that is often the environment of the psychic.

The materialism of most formal religions, and their reliance on scaring people into the paths of righteousness, are equally distracting. The idea of a God who would condemn his children to an eternity of hellish torment must be discarded if we are to seek spiritual harmony. Most people who are drawn to the study of metaphysical Truth have already been subjected to the dogmas and structures of such religions and are ready to put them aside in favor of the simple and demonstrable benefits of metaphysics.

"I AM": Words of Creative Power

*W*hen you think, feel, write or speak the words "I AM," you immediately awaken a vital energy within you—the energy of creation, evoked by a child of God.

The words "I AM" are sacred to God. (To proclaim Himself to man, he used the all-encompassing phrase, "I am that I am"—I am the Creator.) When these words are spoken, the universe stands ready to obey you. In metaphysics, this proclamation of self is a proclamation that you are of God, endowed with His creative powers. "I AM," in metaphysics is the name of God, and a declaration of our higher self, our kinship with the Creator, of His presence within us. It is a statement which must never be used with a negative decree (for this would be a denial of God), but only as a prelude to doing good: The transmutation of a bad situation, the expression of goodwill, of blessing, of forgiveness—of the Truth, which is one of God's aspects.

The Gospel of St. John begins with some of the most poetic and meaningful language in the New Testament:

> *"In the beginning was the Word, and the Word was with God, and the Word was God.*
> *"The same was in the beginning with God.*
> *"All things were made by him; and without him was not anything made that was made.*
> *"In him was life; and the life was the light of men.*
> *"...And the Word was made flesh, and dwelt among us."*

The word is "I AM." First person, singular of "to be." The declaration of self, of creativity personified. Whoever uses it, knowing the power it has is with God, is God at the moment he or she uses it—and nothing in creation can deny the words that follow. "I AM" is the mantra that eases you into the spiritual state, the prelude to your prayers, meditations and treatments.

But the words that follow must be carefully chosen to invoke that perfection and harmony you have declared the right to. And once your treatment is completed, when you achieve your heart's desire, your miracles, never mention the problem or situation again. It has been remedied; bringing it up again will do just that: Bring it up again. You must abandon the habit of telling others, "You just can't imagine what I went through…" or indulging in negative prayers, such as, "Lord please never let that happen again." Things that are figurative in the earthly plane are often literal in the spiritual plane; thus, in reconstructing the situation, you are literally rebuilding it, on the spiritual level—and it is above, so it is below. The phrase "opening old wounds" is truer than most people realize, and the relapse can be even worse than the original condition.

To avoid this pitfall, I recommend the following treatment:

"I AM the creator, the word and the life of the constructive decree I have made regarding this situation, and I forgive myself for allowing any possible relapse through any thoughtless words. I AM the law of forgiveness, and transmuting flame for all errors I have made and for all errors made by any other. I have power because I AM with God. Thank you, Father, for having heard me."

The power to create is yours. Like any power, it must be wielded with judgment and caution. And the words that follow "I AM" must be chosen with special care, for the day are the words of creation.

I AM... *Perfect*

Say it: "I AM perfect." It sounds like the ultimate in egocentricity—but it is a statement that can be made in complete humility and honesty. It is the purest affirmation of loyalty to God, to the Christ within us, to our higher self.

Still, there will always be some who will feel that such a statement is ridiculous. Their consciences rebel, and they feel it is impossible to say this with any honesty. If you feel this way, please remember that this is your earthly "carnal" conscience reacting. The conscience that is an artifact of the parental, religious and cultural values you have been surrounded by since birth; the conscience that looks at man's atrocities, from lies and deceit to murder and warfare, and holds you to be partly to blame because you are member of the human race. This earthly conscience is a necessity if we are to interact with our fellow humans in an ethical manner—but it cannot make judgments on the spiritual level.

And "I AM perfect" is a statement of spiritual Truth. You know that perfection is the natural state of the spiritual plane. You know as well that your higher self exists on the spiritual plane, and is part of that perfection. Furthermore, you know that you are child of God, who is perfection, and that you are created in His perfect image. How, than, could this statement be anything but the most obvious of Truth?

The only way this statement could be untrue is if you make it untrue, with your own denial. Never forget that the power of words works both ways! The power of creation is also the power of destruction. Say that you are less than perfect (or that you are unattractive, that you are hopelessly neurotic, etc.), and you will quickly find yourself living up to (or down to) that self-imposed image.

Do not deny your imperfection—affirm it! If you find instant perfection just too grandiose (despite your spiritual perfection and your kinship with God), then start by saying: "I AM potentially perfect, potentially divine, because this is God's will for me." This should hold your guilt-oriented earthly conscience at bay, and soon you will be able to make the transition to the simple Truth. Use this affirmation often, especially when a bad temper or a state of depression comes over you. You will elevate your consciousness with these words (always a desirable state) and you will experience a growing sense of well-being and euphoria as the Truth sinks in.

You are perfect. Why fight it?

Meditation

*T*here are four stages in meditation, like four galleries in a museum, each leading to the next.

The first stage is the Image. Let's assume that you are meditating on your inner Christ. You have in your mind no more than a fuzzy, shapeless thought, purely abstract. Concentrate on your subject for 20 seconds.

After that first 20 seconds, something new, different and more satisfactory begins to make itself felt. There is no visual picture yet, merely a feeling, the edge of understanding. This is called the Ideal. Let this feeling wash over you for another 20 seconds.

In this time, that sensation becomes clearer, stronger, more expansive. It is the Unification of your thoughts and sensations. If you had to put it into words, you might say something like, "I AM entering a larger place, purer and more open. There are beings here, but I can't see them. I can only feel the love that flows between them and binds me to them."

After another 20 seconds, you enter that fourth room, into a feeling euphoria, soothing peace and satisfaction. You will very likely find yourself smiling, and your face will feel warm with an inner radiance. This is the Realization. The idea on which you have been meditating has merged with your being.

As you can see, this is not an intellectual process, with neatly printed definitions and precise conclusions. It is a process of feeling, or reaching out and touching Truth. Yet it takes no more than the sixty seconds or so I have just outlined to put yourself in touch with God. If you have the concentration and patience to keep your mind focused on only one idea as I have suggested, you will experience the steps very much as I have described them.

Dr. Emmet Fox says: "Don't analyze God's love; feel it." And I hope the above does not sound analytical—however this description of the stages of meditation was great help to me, and I hope it will be useful and convenient for you.

Now you can understand why Dr. Fox says that we can establish communication with God even in the middle of Times Square. You need not isolate yourself in total solitude; in fact, it's probably not wise to get accustomed to such a serene approach: The times when you need God's presence the most might be in the middle of a crowded shopping mall—or an earthquake.

Whatever the circumstances, turning your thoughts to God will bring you a calm, loving silence that blocks out the surrounding turmoil. It is that inner peace that is an intimate moment alone with God.

The Voice of your Soul

*I*t's a common belief that God has a place, a destiny for each of us, and unlike so many common beliefs, it's quite true. Dr. Fox says that our only real problem in life is finding our right niche in life, and when we do, everything else falls into place. Health and happiness. (The two are inseparable.) Prosperity and complete freedom. (Poverty is the enemy of freedom, and vice-versa.) Wealth alone won't do it. Neither will fame and honor. Because, unless you have found the role that is distinctly yours in this life, all the money in the world won't be able to fill the gap of that sense of incompletion.

The universe is the physical and spiritual construction of the Divine Plan. It is unified harmony and perfection. Within this Plan, nothing superfluous or unwanted can exist. And that includes you. You are here; therefore you have a place and a purpose, as distinct and unique as your fingerprints. (God doesn't repeat himself—because He does everything right the first time.) This means the space reserved for you cannot be occupied by anyone else. And this is why rivalries should not exist (and do not, on the spiritual plane): There is only one person truly suited to any position. Rivalries do exist simply because the parties involved are still searching for their proper niches.

The question is, how do we know what our own, personal, custom-tailored niche is? The answer is that most of us already know. Most of us harbor a secret desire. Maybe it's to be an inventor, a writer, a dancer, a senator. And maybe your present life is a dull and unsatisfying stale bread. And maybe you are cursing fate because a crippled leg has made a dancing career a foolish fantasy; or a lack of education, or lack of facility with words or conceptual ideas makes writing or inventing a forlorn hope. It may just be that those secret wishes, your "heart's desires," are guiding you in a general direction, but not toward the specific conclusion you have jumped to. Think of the choreographer whose work outlives the dancer who may perform it. The literary agent or editor, whose recognition of talent can build careers for many writers. The engineer who can take a new idea and make it economically practical. The possibilities are endless, and there are thousands of cases just like these where people have found success and happiness in positions where their dreams and their abilities came together in a perfect blend. Never think your "heart's desire" is impossible for you. It is the voice of your soul that expresses this wish. And God wants you to have it. He will guide you to it, if you let Him.

So don't make excuses: You don't have the right background or education, or talent. Your family obligations are too pressing. It's too late to start now. If you express the negative, the negative will seize dominance, and you will end up with nothing but frustration. And if you frustrate yourself, you frustrate God as well. Even if you are reasonably successful at what you now do, and you still feel that emptiness, you must use scientific prayer to express your faith that what you truly want will come to you—and use every other means in your power to help make it happen. By forcing yourself into a niche that doesn't fit, you are subjecting your soul to uncomfortable distortion.

Remember, when you pray for guidance, God not only shows you the way, he pays the traveling expenses as well, in whatever currency it takes: Training, money, fortitude and opportunity. All you need to do is join your will to His.

Because the voice of your soul—expressing your heart's desire—is the voice of God. And that is a voice that must be obeyed.

Earthly and Spiritual Values

*W*e're scrambling to get ahead, to make a fortune, to do the best can for our families. Worldwide, we seem to have developed what I call a "robbery mentality" in our everyday dealings with others. When a client or associate is financially well off, we tend to think, "He can afford it—let him pay." We don't stop to think that he may well have financial obligations in proportion to his means. Conversely, as customers ourselves, we adopt the attitude that we'd better keep a close eye on the next person, because he's out to take us for all he can. And when we see people who are naturally giving and generous, or who have an incomprehensible tendency to view their fellow men as trustworthy, we think of them sneeringly as hopelessly naive, simple-minded, or just plain suckers.

It's a sad state of affairs. This is the kind of thinking that allows crime and cheating to exist, that makes us think that accusation tantamount to guilt and that someone found not guilty of a crime has "gotten away with it." (Note that verdicts are delivered as "guilty" or "not guilty"—both negative terms. The word "innocent" seems to have been forgotten.)

There are those—usually of the retirement-age generation—who declare that crime and immorality are at their highest peak today, and things were surely different when they were young. But I suspect that things are pretty much the same today as they were when some shaggy cave-to-cave entrepreneur traded a handful of flawed flint spearheads for a perfectly good bearskin and grunted smugly over his neighbor's gullibility.

The fact remains that this attitude of constant suspicion leaves us little time to think of anything else. It's state of constant tension that is absorbed by the physical body, and is manifested in any number of physical ills from skin eruptions to ulcers to heart conditions and cancer.

And when these conditions do arise, we take them to a doctor—in the hope that we'll find one who really cares, not one who'll charge an arm and a leg to cure those limbs because he knows you're not in a position to argue, and the insurance company pays for it anyway and because he has a reputation to maintain, a country club to support, a wife to wrap in furs and children to send to prestigious schools. Not to mention the matching BMWs.

With all this worldly tension and struggle, there's not much time left over for spiritual matters. And even if there were, just developing the ability to shift into a state of elevated consciousness (so directly in conflict with the sheer materialism of the worldly values that have been ingrained into us) would seem to be beyond our abilities.

For people who believe so, it is so. And so many go to their graves, best by stress-related ailments, never having known the possibilities that were open to them, adding new Karmas to old, the older Karmas crystallizing under the pressure of the new. And these dense, diamond-hard Karmas, once freed of their physical homes, remain alive and independent, shrieking the ill-will and error that has produced them into the disembodied ears of their former hosts, and to the universe at large. (A sound that is pure torture top those gifted with psychic abilities.)

Eventually, the disembodied are reborn, bringing their monstrosities with them. Sometimes things work to their advantage, and a violent Karma is placed in a timid framework, bringing about a kind of balance. But the best thing that can happen is for the soul to learn in this next life how to erase the violent Karma forever.

What you learn here (and from your studies in metaphysics in general) will help you face the burdens of your previous existence(s) and learn how to transmute them and dissolve them into light.

The Limits of your Responsibilities

*I*f you are trying to live a spiritual life, you have a right to feel peace in your soul and to enjoy harmonious progress. If there is still turmoil and disharmony in your life, you have the right to know why, to ask the Divine Wisdom for guidance.

First, let's take a look at what are—and what are not—your responsibilities in this life.

It is your responsibilities to devote a reasonable amount of time to daily prayers, whether this takes the form of meditation and scientific prayer, attending a spiritual lecture, reviewing your affirmations or reading books appropriate to your study. You must live your life according to Divine will to the best of your present abilities. If you are fulfilling these requirements, honestly and sincerely, there is really nothing more you can do, and there is no need to reproach yourself because you are not achieving absolute harmony. You are on the road, and you will make progress. And you must accept your limitations. They are only temporary.

For example, it cannot be your duty to try and do something beyond your present strength or scope. God does not ask the impossible of His children.

It cannot be your duty to do that for which your truly have no time. Though the Spiritual world is timeless, God is well aware of the temporal limitations he built into His physical universe and the mortal bodies that people it. You need not deny yourself to your loved ones, forsake the pleasures God made for you on this plane. Your challenge is to make the most of this existence, not to turn your back on it!

It cannot be your duty to accomplish something with money you do not have. If you are facing such a situation, something has gone awry with your thoughts; you may be thinking that God is cruel to place you in situation with your hands tied, forcing you to face certain failure. Remember the 46th Psalm, which begins: "God is our refuge and our strength, and a very present help in trouble." and ends: "Be still, know that I AM God." Repeat this, as an affirmation. You must say it with conviction, in complete faith, because it is your faith that will move mountain. Ask for what you need, and do not attempt the impossible until you have the wherewithal that makes it possible.

It cannot be your duty to do anything that will sacrifice your own integrity or jeopardize your spiritual advancement. No one in the world can force you to lie, for instance, or to accept a lie (which is a form of lying to yourself). When you have doubts, examine that situation in the light of meditation. Your own honesty will bring you the answer. Good actions in an untrue cause are not good actions at all. There is no need to seek for things to do; they will come to you. And there will be plenty of days when there is nothing for you to do but enjoy being alive.

It cannot be your duty to do today what is meant to be done tomorrow. This isn't "putting off"; it's scheduling. In the Spiritual world, there is no past or future; only the present. (This is why you express your wishes as though they have already been granted.) But the physical world doesn't operate by these principles, and neither can you. Today's needs have been met. Tomorrow will present you with another today. You can always plan ahead—but you can do ahead. It cannot be your duty to fulfill a distant obligation by sacrificing one closer to home. In other words, don't give food to a needy stranger if it will take food out of your children's mouths. (This isn't a sacrifice on your part, but on your children's.) The same goes for your time: Your family comes first. The Sermon on the Mount tells us to remove the speck in our own eye before trying to remove one from our neighbor's. In other words, first things first.

Finally, it cannot be your duty to be hurried, sad, depressed, angry, resentful or antagonistic at any time. These are crippling emotions, brought about by personal worries. If you are experiencing them, it's another way of telling you that you still have speck in your eye. Problem-solving through meditation and scientific prayer will clear your vision.

You have one duty, if it comes down to that, and this is to be happy. This is the purpose of metaphysics: To provide you with the practical formulas for achieving this by recognizing your one-ness with God.

It is my duty to wish you all the happiness that God intends you to enjoy. And I hope that this book, and the others in this series, will ease your journey toward perfect harmony. My love goes with you.

Book III

The Mystical Number 7

Introduction

Almost since the day when man first developed the concepts of numbers and counting, certain numbers have taken on a greater significance than others, and foremost among these is the number seven.

Consider the many appearances the number seven makes in everyday life. There are seven days in the week, seven days in the "week" of Biblical creation. There are seven distinct colors in the visible spectrum (red, orange, yellow, green, blue, indigo and violet), seven notes in the standard musical scale, seven ages of man, seven months of pregnancy before a fetus is developed enough to survive outside the womb.

There is a sense of completeness, of fulfillment, of a wheel come full circle about the number seven. The seventh day is the day of rest. Blue shades through violet to become red, in the spectral wheel. The eighth note of the musical octave is the first note repeated in a higher frequency. The number seven governs the sequences of conception to viability, birth to death. The artist's rule of thumb is that the height of a person is roughly seven times the height of the head, from chin to crown.

These are just a few of the most obvious and best known ways in which this remarkable number affects our lives. In this book, I'll be acquainting you with some of the subtler and lesser known manifestations of the number seven, and how they will affect your own personal development and spiritual evolution.

I take it for granted that you are reading these books in sequence, that you have studied and put into practice the principles laid out in the first two books in this series, entitled Metaphysics for Everyone and Your Heart's Desire. If you have not, you will miss many references made in this book. The series is planned as a gradual and cumulative teaching process, and each book is built on the knowledge and principles which the reader has assimilated and employed from the previous one.

There is a maxim that says: "When the Student is ready, the Teacher (Master) will appear." If you have followed the guidelines of the books in the series so far, you are ready for the "Teacher" you now hold in your hands.

CONNY MÉNDEZ

The Brotherhood of Saint-Germain

The Brotherhood of Saint-Germain is the name of a group devoted to the study of Metaphysics, founded by me in Caracas, Venezuela in 1945.

The name derives from the Ascended Master, Comte de Saint-Germain, considered the reincarnation of Vishnu and ruler of this new era, which has been called "The Golden Era of Saint-Germain." We believe in the teachings of the Masters of Wisdom, the Great White Fraternity.

These teachings are purely metaphysical, handed down by the Ascended Masters themselves, explained in terms understandable to the Western mind, and adapted to the standards of contemporary life as it is lived in the Aquarian Age, which began in 1954.

The Brotherhood of Saint-Germain does NOT practice or recommend so-called "Spiritism," or attempts to communicate with the astral sub-planes. We do NOT recognize "Black Magic," nor do we subscribe to any magical practices, or any other doctrine or activity that attempts to subvert free will or is contrary to the full and conscious agreement of any Child of God. We do NOT practice rites or ceremonies. We do not recommend special disciplines or diets other than those consistent with established principles of good health and common sense.

The Brotherhood of Saint-Germain has a free school. Proceeds from the sale of its "texts" and reference books and small voluntary

donations almost exactly equal the reprinting costs of these volumes—
so we may safely be referred to as a non-profit organization.

Our instruction consists, first and foremost, of the awareness and
practice of the Presence of God and the Law of Mentalism, which
we have mentioned before. Once the student has demonstrated an
understanding of these points, we then proceed to teach him or her
to dissolve and transmute his/her karma on this plane, here and now,
without sacrifice or pain, through the application of the Violet flame—
the gift and talent brought by the Ascended and Most Beloved Master
Saint-Germain to his Ministry.

Joining the Brotherhood of Saint-Germain is simplicity itself:
Your desire for metaphysical understanding is all the credential you
need, and the study of the first two books in this series will prepare
you for that understanding. Armed with desire and your increasing
awareness, you'll find yourself experiencing new and positive aspects
in your life. (Here I must warn against consulting or being influenced
by those who practice or advocate Black-Magic or other misguided
rituals, who try to determine the future or change their lives by means
which are not of God. Such mediums or practitioners work through the
manipulation of Lies, Hate and Revenge, as opposed to living in, for
and with the purest and most disinterested Love, which is God's way,
and is the only "magic" needed by the Brothers and Sisters of Saint-
Germain. Furthermore, you do not need to know the future, nor do you
need to change the course of events, since you will be the sole creator
of your future, and you will be creating the future that is best for you
through your actions and prayers.

If you wish to understand beforehand the normal, everyday state
of a metaphysician, read Psalm 91. I urge you to memorize it, as a
guideline; you'll find it most useful in many situations. (The following
opening sentence is omitted in some translations, and should be
memorized as well: "He that dwelleth in the secret place of the most
high shall abide under the shadow of the Almighty.")

The Lord's Prayer

*O*ne prayer is a common link between all the Christian religions, and its fundamental thoughts exist in the other major religions as well. It is the Lord's Prayer, composed and given to us by Jesus with the specific purpose of effecting a radical change in our souls and lives. The Master Emmet Fox says that it is more than a prayer: It is a concise formula for spiritual development.

The prayer consists of seven parts or clauses. Let's examine it, part by part:

First clause: Our Father who art in Heaven...

When you pronounce these first two words—Our Father—you declare that your father is also the father of all, that we are all brothers and sisters. You are praying for others as well as yourself and you are fulfilling the Law of Love in so doing, because all that your ask for yourself, you ask for all your brothers and sisters.

Every father worthy of the name tries to keep his children from suffering and looks after those children's well-being to the best of his abilities and in proportion to his means. Thus, our heavenly Father, having at his disposal infinite love and infinite means, will provide us with infinite protection against adversity, and offers us as his legacy the joy and comfort of the Kingdom of Heaven.

Just as the child molded after the parent, we are made in the image of God, and so we share the Divine Spirit, with all its gifts and powers; we live as children of Heaven in a state of grace. (Helping you toward that discovery is the purpose of these books.) Our world, the world we live in, is the analog of the perfection we call Heaven—or it can be, if we make it so. And we can do so without becoming martyrs or ascetics, but in the joy of life. This world is a part of our Fathers bequest, and is to be enjoyed. Our only obligation is to live in His grace, and to give thanks by saying, with full understanding, this prayer every day.

Second clause: Hallowed be Thy Name...

We give God many names—Jahweh (or Yahweh), Jehova, El, Allah—that we may address Him in prayer. But the only name he has given us is I AM (in saying to Moses, "I am that I am.") These words cannot, therefore, precede any negative statement. When you say, "I AM," you are also affirming your own legacy of Godhood. Thus a negative statement following this declaration would be a lie—a lie which would manifest itself in your own condition, as a result of denying the perfection of God which lies within you.

Thus, when you pronounce the four words of the second clause, you affirm your status as a child of God, wishing yourself and your brothers and sisters the blessings of the name of God, as you bless His name yourself. As you bless God's name, you bless your own!

Third clause: Thy Kingdom come; Thy Will be done, on Earth as it is in Heaven...

It is true that the will of the perfect Father toward His children is perfection, that nothing interferes with the realization of their wishes for happiness. But it is also true that guidance, not force, is the best teacher: A child must stumble in learning how to walk; he or she is not a puppet but a distinct and individual creature, learning to control his or her own muscles and reactions. The child learns through practice and observation, through the loving advice and example of the parent. We have all learned—through sometimes-painful experience—that your parents do not talk just to hear themselves or to annoy us. They do so to warn and advise us, to preserve us from harm and lead us to happiness—and God's will is to lead us to the perfection that is the kingdom of Heaven, by showing us how to create a life that can be heaven here on earth. So, when we say, "Thy kingdom come," we are asking for the guidance that will bring that heavenly state of perfection to us in our daily lives, that God's will literally be done on earth, as well as in heaven.

Fourth clause: Give us this day our daily bread.

Bread means many things. For years, "bread" (not to mention "dough") was slang for money. It obviously means food, sustenance, and as such it stands for the necessities of life, whatever we need to carry us from this day to the next. But, to carry the analogy a little further, bread goes stale after one day. That's why we only ask for this day's, today's bread. We know that tomorrow's will be forthcoming as well. We have only to ask. Because it is "our daily bread," and it has already been granted us, all of us. And in asking, we show our awareness and assurance that we—all of us—will be granted what God has already ordained as ours. This clause is a succinct expression of one of the basic prayers of metaphysics: "Father, you have already decreed that I should have this. I wish for it under Your Grace, in harmony for all, and in a perfect way. Thank you, Father, for I know that you have heard me."

Everything we wish or need has been granted to us even before we ask it. Our asking, our prayer, is only the key that releases our wishes into our waiting hands and hearts.

Fifth clause: Forgive us our trespasses as we forgive those who trespass against us.

If you feel you have nothing to be forgiven for, you may as well stop reading, fold your hands and wait for that high-ranking position that surely awaits you in paradise. If you feel you're not quite perfect, or that it might be a slightly longer wait than you expected, please read on.

We are not simply asking for forgiveness in this clause; we are asking for the justice of the Law as well, and it is a two-edged sword. First of all, whatever our trespasses, debts, sins or whatever we call them, they are forgiven instantly. "A sin admitted is a sin forgiven." God holds no grudges. But His Law makes forgiveness conditional: You are forgiven for your wrongdoing—just as you forgive those who have wronged you. As you deal with others, so you will be dealt with. Your forgiveness is a fact, but you will never truly feel its comfort unless you have forgiven all others in advance.

If you feel that things are going wrong in your life, that you must make monumental efforts to achieve the slightest gain, don't blame it on bad luck. There's no such animal. All luck is of your own creation—a reflection of how you treat the world, and those you share it with. If you examine your actions, you will find that you are too harsh in your judgments of others, too grudging in praise, reluctant to forgive and quick to blame your ill fortune on others. A change in attitudes will change your so-called "luck." And it begins with forgiveness. Each night, make this statement a part of your bedtime ritual—and make sure that it is completely, absolutely sincere: "I forgive all who need my forgiveness, every man, woman and child. I forgive myself, and I ask the Father for His forgiveness."

Do so with total honesty, not holding an iota of resentment for real or imagined wrongs. For resentments build a wall between you and God, between you and all manifestations of happiness, prosperity and inner peace.

You make this a nightly ritual, or you may say it once with the utmost sincerity, so that when a resentment rears its head, you may conquer it by saying, "I already forgave." (If your resentment has to do with work, you might say, "I forgave at the office!")

Sixth clause: Lead us not into temptation, but deliver us from evil.

This is a puzzling concept to many: Why would God lead us into temptation? The answer is that He wouldn't—but, in "leading" us (guiding us) in our evolution, He allows us to walk a path of ever increasing and ever more subtle forms of temptation—the greatest example of which is that toward spiritual pride, the most difficult barrier between you and God. Jesus had a most effective saying to contravene the growth of such pride: "I am tame, and humble of heart." In short, we are asking our Father to lead us past temptation in our evolutionary growth—and to deliver us from any evil we may fall into through our own devices or weaknesses. And we have the assurance that to ask is to be granted what we ask: The Bible tells us, "If the son asks the Father for bread, he will not be given a snake."

God delivers us from evil by showing us—allowing us to realize—that evil is unreal, that it has no place in the Perfect Harmony. But we must beware of subtlety: It has been said that the greatest sins are those of which we are not conscious. The drift toward pride is a gradual and imperceptible one. By asking God to make us aware of our unseen flaws, we can avoid this and other errors, and be delivered from evil.

Seventh clause: For Thine is the Kingdom, the Power and the Glory, forever.

This is the ultimate affirmation—that God alone rules and controls the universe, that to Him alone goes all glory, and that this truth is unchanging for all time. These words are designed to keep us from spiritual pride—the very pride that led to the fall of Lucifer, once the most favored of angels. Whether we take this as allegory or not, it remains a clear and constant warning of the peril of pride. When we say these words, let us do so with total sincerity.

The Seven Aspects of God

*L*et us define the difference between science and religion by saying that science represents divine wisdom and religion represents divine love. Yet there is no difference. Just as that which we call God, or the Creator, is a singularity, one and indivisible, so is all of creation one with its Creator—and with itself. What we see as differences are but manifestations: Science and religion are expressions of the same knowledge. (To paraphrase Arthur C. Clarke: Any science sufficiently advanced is indistinguishable from magic.)

What, then, are the aspects of the one God? They are: Life… Love… Truth… Intelligence… Unity… Spirit… Principle. (In my first book, I use term "Unity" to refer to "Soul." The terms may be considered interchangeable).

God is Life.

God is everywhere; life is everywhere. As God is indestructible, so is Life: What we call death is merely a transformation to another aspect of existence.

And those other aspects are infinite. God isn't a kindly old man with a long white beard; He is indefinable. And He is all life, from the simplest protozoon to the seed that produces a tree, to the self-awareness that is man, and beyond, to the other life forms that inhabit this unmeasurable universe—many of which we would not even recognize as life. There may be creatures that live so slowly—or so fast—that our earthbound senses would not be aware that life on other planes requires no physical structure at all.

Life, whatever its form (or lack of it) does not end: It evolves. And evolution itself is unending, for the ultimate being is the Creator, and when life is taken into the being of God, that is not an end, but a beginning—for God is not only the "omega" of Life, He is the "alpha," the fount from which all life begins.

Life is invisible, as is its Creator. We see its manifestations—from the dividing of an amoeba to the birth of an Einstein-to-be but we cannot (at least at this stage of our existence) see its essence, which is God. So, when we speak of Life, we must speak of life as we know it.

The truth of Life is threefold: Health, happiness and enthusiasm. These three aspects add up to well-being. And it is for this truth—the beating of our hearts, the pleasure in the smile of a loved one, the anticipation of being and doing that come with every new day—that we must thank the Creator with every breath.

We should meditate about Life, because by doing so, we manifest it more fully, building our health, happiness and enthusiasm through our awareness of the perfection of Life. Through this meditation, we become aware that illness, misery and despair are lies: They are anti-life, and are only reflections of our own faltering belief in the Truth. The Bible says, "God's happiness is my strength." It's true: Reflect on the fact that God cannot know sadness, for sadness cannot exist except in direct contradiction of God; if there is no sadness in God, then there can be no sadness in you—for you are of God.

The same is true of your health. Metaphysics does not deny physicians their due: They are trained to heal the faltering body—but if the spirit cannot heal itself, the best doctors can do little to help, for what they treat are symptoms of a spiritual sickness. As you progress in your studies, meditations and evolution, you will discover how to cure you ills. The highly-evolved will also be able to cure the ills of others, by convincing them of the Truth of Life.

It is not wishing that makes it so: it is knowing.

God is Love.

You've undoubtedly heard this phrase before, more or less accepting it without too much thought. But it is a statement meant to be taken quite literally. Love exists, like life, without tangible essence, and is visible only through its manifestations—the feelings you cannot deny, the feelings and actions of others. And the source of these feelings, their essence, is God. (In fact, it can logically be stated that no one who has ever felt love can be an atheist: If you believe in love, you believe in God by believing in one of His aspects, whether you're aware of it or not. In fact, if you believe in good as opposed to evil, that is sufficient. Jesus said, "Do not call me good. There is only one good, and that is God.")

Good is in the majority. We consider that the number seven is the key number in the universe (as this book attempts to demonstrate) and that this prime number is composed of three negative and four positive elements. Thus, the good always outweighs the bad. Positive (plus, or true) is existence; negative (minus, or false) is nothingness. The universe exists, and we exist within it. (Even "empty space" is not a perfect vacuum: There are atoms of hydrogen throughout this so-called emptiness; photons, the particles that make up light, stream steadily in every direction from every star. When we say that nature abhors a vacuum, it's another way of saying that God does not permit absolute nothingness.)

And since good is dominant, we are given the advantage over evil. By simply blessing the good in any situation, however unpleasant or evil the circumstances may appear, we cancel the bad. It's a process as simple as subtracting three negatives from four positives: We are left with one positive, which is the manifestation of good.

It is love, the love of good, which can turn a situation around. By simply saying, "I bless the good in this situation, and I ask that it be shown to me," you have reaffirmed the positive. Similarly, if you feel a person harbors ill will toward you or intends to harm you in any way, say to him or her silently: "I surround you with my circle of love." You are surrounding that person with God—and evil intentions, as they say, don't have a prayer. Surround your home, your loved ones, every aspect of your life with this same circle of love and no true harm can come to you or yours. Your good will (which is, of course, love) will triumph in every situation. Simply remember to apply this formula whenever it is needed.

Love, like all the aspects of God, is within you, merely waiting to be made manifest. You'll find, as you use this and other formulas in your daily life, that your own appearance, your self-manifestation, will change. It will probably be more obvious to others than to you, because that same good will, the God-ness, you have always had within you will have risen to the surface.

This is true of all people. The higher self, the "Christ" within us, is only waiting to be summoned. All the aspects of God are there. A human being is not inherently evil, as some would have us believe, because all humans carry God within them.

St. Paul said, "You are transformed through your mind's renewal." This renewal is achieved by declaring the Truth of Divine Love that is within you. You do this not only by putting that love into words when you have nullified another's ill feelings or actions against you; you must harbor no ill will of your own, you must not bear any grudge or wish for that person's punishment. You must not think of anyone as deserving punishment. You do not hate a child for breaking a valuable object. "Abhor the act, not the child."

By the same token, don't condone wrongfulness in others—or in yourself—in the name of forgiveness. Patting someone on the head and telling him or her, "That's all right; it doesn't matter" is quite different from forgiving; it makes you an accomplice in the wrongdoing, and does the other harm rather than good. Forgiving is love; condoning is indifference.

Negative criticism, condemnation and fear are destroyers, and they keep your prayers from being answered. If you find that nothing positive is happening as a result of your prayers, it's likely that you are harboring a resentment against someone or some situation; you are not acting in accordance with Divine Love.

Love is more than feelings. It is sharing, trying to understand others, being faithful to them and to yourself, to wish others the good fortune you want for yourself, to enjoy beauty, to show good will and consideration, to be patient, to see the other's point of view, to smile— in short, to find and act on the good in every person and situation. (A Biblical story tells that Jesus and the apostles came upon the decomposing body of a dog while walking. The apostles covered their noses and eyes to avoid the stench and sight of death. Jesus merely commented, "Not even pearls are whiter than its teeth." To love is not only to see the good, but also to teach it.)

Love is not giving alms in the street, giving your all to anyone who asks. It isn't your duty to "fix" other people's lives. Moving along your own personal evolutionary path is job enough for any individual—and bringing out the love within yourself will benefit all around you. Your lack of fear will inspire courage in others. Your forgiveness will allow others to forgive. Your own happiness, health, appreciation of beauty and love of all that is life will elicit the same responses in all who come in contact with you. This is Love.

God is Truth.

Truth is many things. It is the truth of a situation—the solution of a crime, the answer to a mathematical question, the time of day, the knowledge of how to produce energy from atomic fusion. These are relative truths, facts, relying on the knowledge of other facts for their discovery. Then there is the beauty of a painting, the unquestioning love of a child, the majesty of a centuries-old tree, the scent of flowers in a breath of crisp autumn air. These are absolute true, living entities in themselves. They are the gestures of God.

If there is a single word defining Truth, it is perfection. All truths are a part of the absolute Truth that is God, just as all forms of love are parts of Divine Love. So, if you are at fault in a given situation, declare that truth. You will be calling on God, and He will show His Truth—and people will change their attitudes from blame to understanding, and the situation will be resolved. Your truth invokes God's forgiveness. And if another is at fault, do not proclaim it; instead, ask for God's truth to be shown. You will find that the situation will resolve itself to your benefit.

The ultimate Truth is perfection: The resolution of a situation, the restoration of perfect harmony; for this is the order, the Law, of God's universe.

God is Intelligence.

We call God omniscient, or all-knowing. Intelligence is the comprehension and use of knowledge. A person with a photographic memory may know every word on a page he has just read—and still not understand the concepts those words express. Intelligence is the highest form of awareness (sentience), and it is possessed in varying degrees by every animal, plant and stone, every creation in the universe, right down to the basic building blocks of the atom. Meditate on the nature of things and you will realize than everything responds, everything acts and is acted upon. A mountain responds to wind and rain, rocks tumble and crumble themselves into sand to become deserts or beaches. The electron responds to its nucleus and becomes the smallest component of an element; atoms cluster according to universal laws and become molecules, and molecules make up everything from a star's blazing furnace to the spiraling ribbons of DNA—and can anyone tell us at what point that mysterious condition we call 'life' enters into the picture?

In the broad sense, life is within everything, for intelligence cannot exist without it.

In metaphysics, we act on this assumption. And it works.

Does a situation have life? A child does. So does a pet or a plant. But what about an automobile? Or an electrical appliance? If they do, they have some share of the intelligence that is God.

Test it for yourself. When a troublesome situation arises in your life, when a child will not behave, a pet develops undesirable habits, a plant begins to wither, the car won't star or the toaster turns out charcoal instead of toast—speak to him, her or it. Remind it that it is a part of God, that it has a share of His universal Intelligence, and that it was meant to be a part of the perfect harmony of the universe, and that your life, too, is included in that perfect harmony. You may be surprised to find that this treatment works—and even more surprised to find that it works better on a recalcitrant appliance than on a stubborn child! (After all, the child has vastly more intelligence, not to mention free will, than your average toaster.)

If we truly believe that God is endowed with every quality of an infinitely, loving, just and all-powerful Creator, He will manifest Himself for us. You may feel that the solution that shows itself is more a result of your own patience, or your reassessment of the situation than anything else—and often, you will be right. But isn't that newfound patience, the understanding that lets you say the right words or turn the right screw the simplest and most direct way for God's intelligence to show itself? You are, after all, one of His instruments. And the harmony you create in your own life you also create for the child, the pet, the plant—and even that grateful slice of bread.

Treatments are words. And we know that words are our most powerful tools. When a child brings home a bad report card, there is a reason, and kind, intelligent words are the only way to discover that reason, and to improve conditions. When you show your willingness to understand, you are manifesting God's intelligence. This is true in any situation: School, work, social interaction, health, finances, life in general. One basic approach covers all: You must bless the intelligence of the person, place, object or situation and ask God to manifest His intelligence and restore the harmony that is His Law. Even the most personal conditions, from obesity to a stammer, depression to poor physical health can benefit from repeated treatments. Speak directly to the condition, to the organs, the very cells involved, reminding them that they are integral parts of your intelligence and God's, and that they must function properly to maintain your personal harmony. It may sound foolish at first, speaking to cells or objects or circumstances, but you must remember that you are speaking to the Creator through one of his manifestations—and that your belief, your knowing that you are heard is what makes the treatment effective. Disbelief or half-heartedness will lead to failure.

God is Unity.

It may seem contradictory to talk about the absolute oneness of God, and then to talk about ourselves as individuals or of God as individualizing Himself in various manifestations, but remember, the word individual itself means an indivisible part, and when we consider these parts as separate entities it is only a way of focusing our attention and energy on an aspect of life in order to restore the whole to harmony.

Similarly, we speak of ourselves as though we were many beings instead of one—the Inner Christ, the carnal self, the Higher Self, conscience, body, mind and so forth. Even when we use the word 'I', we are usually distinguishing ourselves from others, and from God. But this is a way of thinking, for the 'I'—the only 'I' is God. Again, we are merely focusing on one of His aspects. And to believe in oneself is to believe in God. It is this belief, this awareness—this intelligence—that can bring perfect harmony to our lives. And whenever we face a task that seems to large, too fearsome, too overwhelming for us, we must meditate on this unity, and realize that God acts through us, and the path will become smooth. Man is the instrument. God is the moving force. And the two are one.

God is Spirit.

To many religions, Spirit is probably the most familiar, yet the least easily defined aspect of God. Spirit has no substance, no visible form, yet it cannot be destroyed, damaged or diminished. It cannot age, become tired or ill. It cannot die. It does not suffer sin, resentment, depression or disillusionment. Spirit represents a higher plane than the physical. It is not subject to physical weakness, since it is pure essence; rather, it controls the physical. So when you work on the spiritual level, you are controlling physical circumstances.

For you are Spirit. You can never truly die. The material body is not an illusion, any more than the physical universe is. The body exists and deteriorates according to physical laws. It is merely a temporary vehicle, an ambulatory conveyance for the spirit (the true essence of being, of self) during its brief visits to the physical plane. The body is not your Truth but merely an aspect of it, and as such is subject to your spiritual control. That control, the Spirit, is your Truth, and when you achieve a spiritual level while living on the physical plane, you may speak with that spiritual Voice, lovingly, to the very cells of your body, and they will do your bidding—because your spiritual Voice is the voice of God. God has but one command for us, for the universe, and that is the perfection of absolute Harmony.

We have all read stories of—and many of us have experienced— so-called miraculous events. Unexplainable cures, spontaneous remissions, survival under incredible circumstances, amazing occurrences of good fortune. These are not miracles, but examples of spiritual control.

That control begins with prayer (treatments). And it is not limited to your own body. As you advance, you will find that you can exert control over circumstances, the actions of others, even inanimate objects, if your wishes are expressed properly, in keeping with the perfect Harmony that is God's Law. (You will be able to understand this truth more fully—and test it for yourself—if you have read the previous books in this series.)

God is Principle.

A principle is a prime and irrevocable law. Gravity is a function of mass in relation to distance. This is true from the easily observable facts that things fall to earth and that water seeks its own level to the fact that even light cannot escape the incredible gravitational pull of the collapsed stars called "black holes." Science is man's search for the principles that govern the existence and the events of the physical universe. There are four known Forces at work in the universe: Gravitation, electromagnetism and the "weak" and "strong" nuclear forces. Einstein, in his attempt to prove that these four were expressions of a single force (Unified Field Theory), was searching for a way to express what metaphysicians (or should I say metaphysicists?) call the Principle of Harmony. Today's physicists are still struggling with the problem of a Grand Unified Theory. It's a matter of knowing something must be true while searching for absolute proof.

In the meantime, we all go on with our lives within the framework of these immutable laws, working with them to the best of our ability. In a sense, metaphysics is closer to engineering than pure science: We acknowledge the existence of the Principles that govern all things, and we make use of them—even though we may never fully understand them. (In theory, the bumblebee's shape and wing-surface-to-size ratio render it aerodynamically incapable of flight; not being aware of this, the bumblebee blithely buzzes on.)

Simply stated, God is the principle of Perfect Harmony. We cannot change this principle (nor would we want to), but we can embrace it and let it work to our benefit—since our health and happiness are part of that Harmony. Working with this Principle is like tuning a radio: We "turn ourselves on" by achieving a spiritual state; we "tune in" by thinking of God or one of His aspects in connection with the situation at hand, and we communicate with our prayers or treatments.

The Principle is one, just as God is one. Yet Principle, too, has seven aspects. In the next pages, we shall examine these aspects in order to focus more precisely on the aspects of our lives.

The Seven Universal Principles

The Seven Principles are: Mentalism, Correspondence, Vibration, Polarity, Rhythm, Cause and Effect, and Regeneration. I recommend that you memorize this list in the order presented, bearing in mind that this breakdown of Principle is a convenience, and that these Principles act as one. Perhaps the best way to understand this concept is to think of Principle as a seven-sided jar. Each side is distinct, yet each is joined to the others, and without any one of them the vessel would be incomplete—and it wouldn't hold water. Complete, it is a vessel of infinite capacity.

In the process of these studies, you may feel the urge to refute, to argue. For now, I ask that you put aside such urges until you have completed the series. Hold your doubts in abeyance, or they will interfere with your grasp of the total concept. Once you have completed all four books, bring out your arguments. If you have read carefully and applied the Principle involved, you'll find those doubts have dissipated like mist in the morning sun.

The Principle of Mentalism

If you have read the first book in the series, Metaphysics for Everyone, you are already acquainted with the Principle of Mentalism as the most important of the Principles of creation, as an introduction to the Truth that lies behind all things visible and material. The Truth is this: All is Mind. All things are thoughts, and all thoughts are things. The most visible example is the development of a child. Tell him from birth that he is worthless, ugly, stupid and inept, and you will create a cringing misfit of an adult, full of hate and terror. But tell this same child he is loved, he is valuable, intelligent and capable, and you have created a successful, well-adjusted individual who is happy and loving. Those constantly repeated thoughts have become facts.

What you can do with the impressionable raw material of a young child's mind, you can do with yourself, your associates, your surroundings. And you can do it with thoughts and words. All is mind. On the simplest level, a cheerful, pleasant attitude (even at times when you aren't really in the mood) will not only improve your own inner feelings, but will produce the same feelings in those around you as well—with the result that those happier faces around you will build your own sense of well-being even more. (A most un-vicious circle!) The simple thought of happiness, expressed in a smile, is a very powerful tool.

The Principle of Mentalism also tells us that this remarkable positive force has its negative side. If you harbor self-doubts, resentments, ill-will towards others, negative thoughts in general, these too will generate negative feedback from others. (When we get to the section on Vibration, you'll discover that the term "negative vibes" is more than just a catchy phrase from the 1960s.) Positive or negative, your true beliefs will always be manifested.

But do you really know what your true beliefs are? The ones that are often buried in your subconscious? It's sometimes hard to distinguish between what you really believe, what you believe you believe and what you feel you should believe. If you feel, for instance, that "if it weren't for bad luck you'd have no luck at all," you won't find yourself winning big in any lotteries—and gold prospecting is definitely a poor career choice. On the other hand, if you believe you're basically a lucky person, you'll find yourself walking into a job interview the same day that the person in the position you're best qualified for announced his retirement, and generally stumbling over good opportunities at every turn.

Which brings up the fundamental question: Is there really such a thing as "luck" to begin with? Certainly there is—and it's entirely under your control.

The point is, every condition in your life is a manifestation of something you believe—a thought made into reality. But you have free will—the freedom to change that reality for the better. No matter how ingrained your subconscious beliefs may be, they can be changed with meditation and the understanding that the Truth is always positive, always good. It is up to you to let that Truth "make you free."

If you enter a brightly lit room filled with objects of every color and put on a pair of red-tinted glasses, green objects will appear brown or almost black, reds will lighten or disappear entirely, something printed in a light red will be indistinguishable from the surface it's printed on. Try the same thing with green-tinted glasses; other interesting changes will occur. Amazing how the way you look at things can alter your reality, isn't it?

All you have to do is change those mental lenses to bring about the reality you want. And the best lens is one that's absolutely clear; it will give you an unfiltered view of the truth. Because the truth is that everything you want is already yours.

Why doesn't everyone know and practice this Principle? Why is there so much misery, poverty and illness in the world? Logical questions. But this and other principles are not as obvious as they may seem. And the ability to believe utterly, to the point where it is not simply belief but knowing, is not born into us; we must be trained, and even those who have studied metaphysics for years can find it difficult to overcome beliefs that have been pounded into them from infancy. It is like gymnastics: Almost anyone can become a relatively accomplished gymnast if he or she starts while the body is still flexible and follows a regular workout schedule. But how many do so? Very few. Because most don't believe it's possible for them. Because they're busy with other pursuits. Because it just isn't important enough to warrant the effort. Even though they know it would bring them health, pleasure, feelings of accomplishment. It's just too difficult, and most give up after the first fall. (It's a good thing babies don't feel that way about walking.)

But be assured that a life of happiness, health and prosperity are within your reach, if you make the effort. Few of us will ever become a Master such as Hermes Trismegistus or Saint-Germain, but virtually everyone can make his or her life on this earth—and beyond—a joyful experience. We simply have to want it as much as God wants it for us.

The Principle of Correspondence

The Principle of Correspondence (which we covered briefly in the first book of this series) can be simply stated: "As it is above, so it is below; as it is below, so it is above." This means that everything in our earthly environment—every object, person, event or emotion—has its analog or correspondent in all the other planes of existence.

We are given much conflicting information in the course of most religious education. We are to believe in a loving God—and yet this is the same God who condemns us all with a blanket indictment that says, "Man who is born of woman is conceived in sin," and tells us that we must atone for that "sin" throughout our lives. It isn't even our sin, but that of Eve. Putting aside the concept that Adam remains apparently blameless, and that the whole story is more symbolic than historical, common sense tells us that a loving God would hardly hold an entire species to blame for its putative progenitors' error. And why would God want to deny us the fruit from the "tree of knowledge of

Good and Evil" if He want us to avoid evil in our lives? If one is to avoid something, one had better be able to recognize it. (A loving parent doesn't tell a child, "Watch out for the deadly Gziltch!" without at least giving the child a verbal description that will allow him to tell the difference between a gziltch and an ice bucket.) And if God is omniscient, then He must know before the birth of a baby whether or not he or she is doomed to a life of misery, or will be condemned to "eternal hellfire." This isn't loving—it's downright cruel. And common sense tells us God doesn't act in this manner.

And what is the analog of common sense on the spiritual plane? It is Divine Wisdom. The wisdom of which we are a part and which is within all of us. The wisdom that, by its very existence, tells us that God wants us to know good from evil, that he wants us to know everything we are capable of learning. Including how to control our own lives and destinies.

As it is above, so it is below. Another way of saying that we are all analogs of God, though we can no more imagine what it is like to be God than an ant can imagine what it is like to be human. But we can visualize the correspondences, since we are blessed with greater consciousness than the ant. (An ant cannot recognize that man and ant alike build homes and cities and protect them from enemies, have territories and—unfortunately—go to war over their boundaries, and that we both have strict societal structures. We can see these parallels, and apply them to the planes above us as well as those below.)

Many people, walking along the street, will change stride to avoid stepping on a grasshopper. Almost everyone will swerve his car to avoid hitting a small animal. And anyone in full possession of his senses would swerve, slam on the brakes and risk hitting a tree rather than hit a child in the road. These are actions taken without thought, actions born of a reverence for life. For we are created "in the image and likeness" of God; as it is above, so it is below. If we were the creations of an indifferent, uncaring or cruel God, the animal or child would be no more than an irritating obstacle to us, and our only consideration would be the amount of damage hitting them might cause our car.

Recognizing, understanding and making use of these correspondences between the planes is a matter of relative levels of consciousness. There may be animals of a "genius" level capable of seeing parallels between themselves and man. There are certainly people on earth today whose spiritual consciousness is so evolved that are capable of perception on levels other than the material one we occupy. And within this vast universe, there are doubtless many races of beings both above and below us on the spiritual scale, even some who have evolved beyond the limitations of physical existence. (If any interstellar travellers have visited us, they would most likely be of this type: The speed of thought is instantaneous—but physical beings are limited to less than the speed of light.)

The Principle of Vibration

The third Hermetic Principle states that all things have motion, which is another way of saying that all matter has energy. (Einstein took it a step further by showing that matter is energy—and vice versa.) The vibrations of a rock exist primarily on the atomic level, and its potential energy is a function of its mass in relation to gravity— the impact of a falling rock is quite measurable.

Thoughts, too, have their characteristic vibrations and colors, corresponding to the frequencies of the electromagnetic spectrum. (When we speak of vibrational "colors," we are speaking in analogies, as a way of visualizing the invisible.) Positive thoughts have extremely high vibrational frequency, and their colors are brilliant and luminous. Negative thoughts vibrate more slowly and their colors are dimmer, more opaque. The same is true of the vibrational frequencies of the positive and negative spiritual poles. A positive thought, like a mind that is positively polarized, cannot be overwhelmed by a negative one. But when the majority of ideas a person carries within are negative in nature, that person's polarity can become negatively aligned. But there must be a negative core for those negative thoughts to gain a foothold. If you can maintain that positive polarity, there is nothing for negative thoughts to adhere to. Jesus said, "The god of this world comes to me and finds nothing to seize hold of in me." He spoke of Satan, the negative polarity that governs the majority of earthly minds.

Material things, from the atomic level on up, have circular motion. Electrons appear at random in their orbital shells. Planets orbit their suns and galaxies revolve around their galactic centers. The linear force of gravity produces this circular motion through a combination of distance, velocity and relative mass. (The spiritual analog of gravity is, of course, the attraction we call love.)

But there is motion that crosses the barriers between the physical and the spiritual, and this is vibration. Most of us have seen sound waves made visible on the screen of an oscilloscope, with the lowest notes (those with the slowest frequency) having high and wide peaks and valleys and the highest notes appearing almost as a straight line. We use the same analogies to depict the frequencies of the electromagnetic spectrum, from radio waves and microwaves through the narrow band of visible light to X-rays and gamma rays. Spiritual vibrations act in similar ways to those of light. Our emotions are vibrations, with the lower frequencies the most negative and the highest frequencies the most positive, or Godlike. Like light waves, these emotional vibrations can augment each other, such as anger stimulating the same emotion in another human being, or love responding to love. Or they can cancel each other out, by being "out of phase" with each other. The vibrations of good cheer can quickly dispel ill will between people. Prayers, treatments, thoughts of God can do much to cancel out the negative vibrations of illness and unhappiness—and we have all seen how a bitter argument can spoil a pleasant occasion for a room full of people.

Keeping your own thoughts in a pleasant mode by recognizing the good, the beauty of a situation, can go a long way toward maintaining the good mood of others through positive reinforcement.

The Principle of Polarity

This is an expression of the duality of all things, the fact that everything has its positive and negative side, its contradictory elements. And there is a seeming contradiction in the principle as well, though the two poles seem to be diametric extremes, they are in fact the same—and what separates them is a matter of degree. The reason for this is that when we are speaking of poles, we are speaking in terms of something that has no beginning or end: the circle. Take the chromatic spectrum. We say that red and blue are at opposite ends of the spectrum; yet blue shades again into red, through hues of violet and purple. There are no ends to the spectrum, only an endless circle. East and west are only relative terms if we travel to the east for some 24,000 miles, we arrive at our starting point. What we call hot and cold are only measurements of the same thing—temperature—from the absolute zero of space to the millions of degrees at the core a star, we are really measuring various degrees of heat.

The same characteristics are true of the Mental and Spiritual planes. Are love and hate truly opposites? We say these emotions are "two sides of the same coin"—but the operative word here is "same," for love and hate are easily confused, and both are measurements of degrees of affection (or emotional attraction, if you prefer.) Fear and valor follow the same rule: Without fear, there can be no bravery, because bravery is not fearlessness but the overcoming of fear. And both extremes are levels of bravery, from paralysis to the burst of action that characterizes a dragonslayer.

What is just as important is the fact that "opposites" can be changed. Love can become hate, misery can be transmuted into happiness, poverty into wealth, sickness into health. And vice-versa.

And this is true because Matter and Spirit (or energy) are also poles, having no more than vibrational degrees of evolution between them. Spirit is the more positive of the two, just as truth is more positive than a lie, love is more positive than hate, knowledge is more positive than ignorance, and motion is more positive than inactivity.

We can change our polarities by meditating briefly on the condition we want changed within ourselves and then strongly on its "opposite." We can turn fear into courage by considering the fact that if fear is in us, then so is courage . . . that courage is the higher, more positive trait . . . and that God's will is for courage, for the most positive aspects in all of us to become dominant. You will soon see the change in yourself, once you have put your wishes into words—and you will also see that you can make these polar changes in others, in the conditions that surround you as well, using the Principles of Mentalism and Vibration. The most general approach in changing others is to recognize, greet and awaken the Higher Self, the Christ-within that exists in your fellow man. This can be done by simply remembering and stating that this Higher Self, this Truth is the Perfection of God (also known as the Immaculate Concept). You will be able to forget the defects in others and concentrate on their positive qualities. Soon those defects will lessen and those positive aspects will strengthen, not only in your own point of view, but in fact.

The positive vibrational frequency of the accomplished metaphysician very often has a profound effect on any environment he enters. His presence alone is sufficient: The confident good will in his eyes, his caring smile and appearance of serenity and happiness serve to polarize all negative mental states around him. With a few positive words, he can change the humor of those around him, transforming despair into hope, anger and frustration into smiles and determination.

The vibrational power of Jesus was so great that he could heal with a touch—reaching out and discovering the Immaculate Concept in others, polarizing the Perfection of God in them to turn illness into robust health. And when he said, "Go and sin no more," he was referring to the error of negative thoughts, words or deeds that had brought illness upon them.

Metaphysicians know that all illness is mental or spiritual in origin, unwittingly created by the individual. We also know that illness can be cured through mental and spiritual treatment. Please note that we do not advocate avoiding doctors or ignoring their advice. They are as much a part of God's plan for your good health as is your spiritual well-being. (Remember, people who have never heard of metaphysics get well under their care!) While the mechanics of establishing good health in yourself are deceptively simple, developing the faith—that absolute sense of knowing that perfect health is, literally, your God-given right—that will accomplish this takes time, study and practice. Relying on the knowledge and skills of your physician is not an admission of your metaphysical ineptness—it's common sense!

The under (or over) lying Truth is that there is no death; there is only Life. Illness, then, is a function of your belief. We have all been taught, to some degree, that we begin dying the day we are born. The process of ageing seems to bear this out. It is difficult to put aside the "facts" we have been taught since early childhood, but it must be done. Let us begin by saying that we begin to evolve from the day we are born, by believing that when we "shuffle off this mortal coil," we do not die, we are moving on to another level of personal evolution. Life is indestructible. Death is misconception. And illness is a byproduct of this misconception, curable by Divine Wisdom (spiritual healing, polarization) and its earthly correspondent, common sense (medical care and good health practices.)

You must first learn to love yourself before you can truly have capacity to love others. The same is true with polarization: You must start with your own persona. Let's take the simplest possible example. The smile is the outward manifestation of well-being, and belongs to the positive pole. The wrinkled brow belongs to the negative pole. When you feel negative vibrations,—sadness, anger, frustration—within yourself, smile. Affirm the good that is within this seemingly negative situation, and add, "I want the good to show itself." In arranging your face into a smile, you have begun the process; your body recognizes this muscular configuration as something connected with happiness, and the rest of your body begins to attune itself to the same positive frequency. You will soon find your spirits lifting, your thoughts considering solutions rather that dwelling on the problems. And your smile will have become more than a muscular exercise; it will be real, because it now comes from the inside.

Just like anything else you wish to master, polarization takes practice. Once you become adept at this, you'll discover that you can create a sense of well-being in others as well. Smiles can be positively contagious.

The Principle of Rhythm

In the section on Vibration, we discussed the inward and unseen oscillations that characterize people, moods, emotions, events and life in general. When we speak of Rhythm, we are talking about the more visible, macroscopic cycles shown by all things and beings. The seasons of the year. The ebb and flow of the tides, the pole-to-pole swing of a pendulum. The repetition of contraction and relaxation of the muscle that sends the lifeblood through our bodies. The predictable cycle of sunspots and solar flares in our sun—and the multibillion-year cycle of an expanding and contracting universe.

Life, "death," rebirth. The fluctuations between the poles. We are subject to all of these tidal rhythms—and we must learn to use them, rather than being overwhelmed by them, just as an aikido master learns to turn his opponent's every motion to his own advantage.

We do this through polarization, using the rhythms in our own lives as a suffer uses the enormous power of a cresting wave, always staying just ahead of its collapse. Once you have acquired a significant measure of spiritual control over yourself, you can develop a rhythm of your own, learning to move with the positive flow and avoid the negative ebb. This is possible because there are two levels of mental processes. The "wave" is on the lower plane, and so we can make use of that positive crest to reach positive polarity—and then elevate our thoughts to the higher mental plane, remaining at that positive pole, while the wave collapses, leaving that negative "undertow" with nothing to hold onto. To use another analogy, it's something like riding a rollercoaster to its highest point and stepping off onto a convenient platform before it begins its downward plunge.

Specific treatments for elevating yourself to the higher mental plane and for positive polarization will be found in all four of the books in this series. Once you understand the principles, however, you will able to create your own treatments of prayers in your own words. Remember—words are powerful, but it is your faith that gives them that power!

The Principle of Cause and Effect

The mind is a dynamo—a source of energy—and thoughts are the energy it generates. Thought energy is expressed in vibrations or waves that, like radar or sonar, return to us, bringing information about the future our thoughts have created.

We have already seen how we "reap what we sow." (The more current terminology is: "What goes around, comes around.") We know that our beliefs as to what will happen, what we are capable of, what other people are like, actually determine those events, create our capabilities and affect the attitudes and actions of others. Thoughts are a powerful form of energy indeed: They do not merely reflect—they create.

So, if you feel ill will toward someone, if you act unfairly or do something that brings physical or emotional harm to another person, your thoughts, words or acts create vibrations of a negative "color" or frequency, and those vibrations attract vibrations of the same "hue," bringing negative events into your life. And these rebounding negative frequencies are doubled in intensity when they return to you. An unkind remark can bring you a minor auto accident. A lie that causes someone to lose a promotion can lose you your job. Adherence to truth and good will are principles that should be adopted simply because they are positive and right—but they are also for your own good!

You reap what you sow. This is part of the system of perfect balance around which the universe is built. You may ask: What happens if someone dies before you can redress a wrong done to him? What about an obviously "evil" person, who has built a fortune on the stolen works and wrecked lives of others, who lives with a beautiful family in kingly luxury? Or the person who has spent his life helping others, who is visited with tragedy and disaster, the death of loved ones and catastrophic illness?

The answers to these and similar questions lie in karma and reincarnation. Universal justice and balance go beyond a single lifetime. Few people are Godly enough to achieve a perfect life on their first try. And God is merciful enough to give you all the chances you need to even things out. Karma is the balance of positive and negative vibrations you have created at the end of a physical lifetime. The good person who suffers misfortune is someone who is balancing the bad karma of a previous life with his good acts; his misfortunes are the negative vibrations that have followed him to this life. Very likely such a person is ready to evolve toward a higher state of being. The bad person who seems to have nothing but good fortune is reaping the rewards of goodness in a previous life—but he is destroying that positive karma with his bad acts in this life. He will suffer for it, in this life or the next. As for a debt you may owe to one who has left this life, if the debt is a small misdeed, you may erase it by general good works in this life. If the debt is enormous, one that has resulted in great unhappiness, both your future lives will be entwined: Such vibrations are said to be "in phase," and the two of you will be contemporaries in another life, where you will be in a position to set things right— indeed, you will be subconsciously driven to do so in that life. (This vibrational attraction is just as strong for mutual emotions. Those deeply in love—and those with powerful animosities—will find themselves drawn together in subsequent lives as well.)

Reincarnation may seem a radical concept to some, and this is because of our Western reliance on material evidence (though there is a growing body of just such evidence that has convinced many Western minds that reincarnation is fact.) Considering the fact that we live today, that we have a soul we consider to be immortal, is the idea that that soul, that essence, which inhabits several bodies any more outlandish than that it inhabits one? I find it no more unlikely than living in several houses during the course of one earthly life. And there are literally billions of people of various races and religions throughout the world who accept reincarnation as logical and unquestionable truth—and that includes quite a few millions in the "materialistic" Western world who are as thoughtful about their spiritual lives as they are about physical existence.

We have and always will have complete control over the events of our lives. With this knowledge comes the corollary awareness that we are responsible for the bad in our lives as well as the good. What we must avoid at all costs is a sense of blame and the self-destructive feeling of despair that can go along with it. For those feeling act as a decree; your thoughts of blame and self-punishment punishment will become fact, and misfortune will be drawn to you. It is self-forgiveness which you must practice. (One of the values of the Catholic ritual of confession is the absolution it brings. It is not the priest, of course, who forgives the confessor's sins. Nor is it God, who has already forgiven. It is the "sinner" himself.) That self-forgiveness opens the door to undoing your past negative thoughts and deeds with new and positive practices. It is the doorway to good will and perfect Harmony.

The Principle of Generation

The underlying theme of this Principle is that there is a masculine and a feminine side to the beginnings of everything. What is true among the higher-evolved creatures of this physical plane—plants, animals, people—is symbolically true of the higher planes. (As below, so above.) As you can see, both Polarity and Correspondence are involved in this Principle: The Laws are inseparably interwoven to form the seamless fabric of the Universe.

When we speak of masculine and feminine, we are not speaking of sexuality but of the polar components that produce life. Again, we speak symbolically: Science is seen as a masculine component, Religion as feminine; Intelligence is viewed as fatherly and Love as motherly in their roles. And when we speak of religion, we are not speaking of "the church." Religion is a body of beliefs, founded on faith and love; the word church means a convocation of men, and the idea has degenerated into a bureaucracy of laws, ritual, sins and punishments, all of which bear little resemblance to the teachings of such Masters as Jesus or Moses. Religion is personal, individual faith; church is politics—and those who embrace the dogma of a church most fervently are most often those in whom faith is the weakest, for they have not discovered faith for themselves, but have had it handed to them, neatly categorized, laden with canonical "additives" and packaged like a frozen dinner. It is difficult to live by one's religion on such a strict and restricted diet—and those who manage to do so are Godly indeed.

Science proceeds under considerably less restraint (although there is a tradition-bound hierarchical structure in scientific circles). As a result, man's progress in discovering the laws governing this physical universe has been considerably more rapid than religion's (or the church's) understanding of the spiritual realm.

The goal of metaphysics is to reunite science and religion. After all, both grew from early man's curiosity, his desire to understand the phenomena that surrounded him. As such things as lightning, volcanoes, the motions of the planets became explainable in physical terms, these phenomena left the realm of mysteries of the gods and entered the province of man's science.

But science still has its mysteries, and personal religion has its practical side. The great teacher Emmet Fox calls the practical application of religion "scientific prayer," and the books in this series are designed to show you how the laws of the universe are both scientific and religious, and to teach you how to make a practical use of these laws.

And, with the joining of the masculine and feminine components of Life and the Universe, we can generate true understanding of that Universe, and approach the perfection that is its grand design.

The Seven Rays

In the opaque chromatic spectrum, mixing all colors together produces black, but in the light spectrum, all the colors mixed together produce white light; in a prism of glass, or of moisture-laden air, those colors are broken down again into a rainbow. As you know, there are only three primary colors: blue, yellow and red; mixing the primaries in chromatic pairs produces the secondary or complementary colors, green, orange and violet.

When we speak of the colors of the Seven Rays, we must speak analogously, since the Rays are of a spectrum that lies beyond our visual powers. (There are people who are able to see the personal auras of others, but these individuals are seeing on the spiritual level, and the colors they report are those of our visual spectrum, since there is no way of translating what they see into understandable terms.) Thus, we use the principle of correspondence in speaking of the Seven Rays.

According to the Master Saint-Germain, the colored sphere that surrounds the "I AM" or life essence of everyone is the spiritual aura, representing the color vibrations of what we call the Seven Spheres.

Every life on earth is influence by the Ray of one of these spheres which is the first home of that life; however, the individual is not confined to that sphere or ray, and the spirit may visit any sphere or radiate any Ray it wishes. Though the person will find that he or she is drawn to the corresponding color of the Ray of his or her "house."

Note also that when we speak of vibrations in terms of these Rays, we are again speaking in correspondences. The spectrum of audible sounds runs from roughly 16 to 25,000 cycles per second, and represents molecular collisions in the medium through which sound is transmitted, such as air or water. Without such a medium, there is no sound transmission—which is why there is no sound in a vacuum. (Contrary to Hollywood's insistence on having booming explosions in space.) The speed of sound is roughly 750 mph at sea level; in the denser underwater environment, it travels faster and farther. The electromagnetic spectrum, however, is an entirely different class of radiation, and travels at the speed of light—about 186,000 miles per second. There are 81 octaves of frequencies within this spectrum, from the lowest detected micropulsations at .01 cycles per second to more than 100 quintillion (10/20) cycles per second for gamma rays. Of these, only one octave is visible to us: The visible light spectrum from 400 trillion to 800 trillion cycles. But the spectrum of the Seven Rays is still another kind of radiation, traveling at the speed of thought, which is instantaneous, since thought has no physical properties. So if we speak of numbers in terms of the Rays' frequencies, we can only speak of their positions on a relative scale, and assign numbers which are symbolic, rather than metrical in nature.

For example, we speak of the densest rock as vibrating at a frequency of two cycles per second. And we use the term 'octaves' as the physicists do, to mark each doubling of the number of vibrations (and halving of the wavelengths). On this relative scale, then, from the 4th to the 20th octave, or between 16 and 1,048,576 cycles per second. The mental plane falls between the 21st and the 28th octaves. The octave of thought is the 28th. The spiritual plane starts on octave 45. Octave 57 is known as the Octave of Truth, vibrating at 144,115,188, 075,855,872 cycles per second.

The Higher Self "I AM"

We depict the individual as a figure whose head—the seat of consciousness—is surrounded by a great circle made up of seven concentric bands as seen in *The Mighty "I AM" Presence* (image on next page). The figure is your Higher Self, your personal spark of Divinity, and the circle represents the spectrum of your personal aura, your "halo." (Remember, the halo was not simply the fanciful invention of Renaissance artists: It was a representation of eyewitness accounts concerning those highly evolved persons—often called saints—who were able to project the Rays of their personal auras so strongly that they were visible to others.) This Higher Self is also called the Causal Body, and its colors represent all the good and constructive acts you have performed in all your past lives. These good acts can never be negated or destroyed; they are yours by what metaphysicians term "right of consciousness." They are your Truth.

And because you possess this Higher Self, you have the right to proclaim another Truth: "I AM perfect." This is not pride in your earthly accomplishments, but an affirmation of your own Godhood— that you are of God, and that He is within you. With every affirmation of this truth, you bring your Higher and Lower Selves closer together.

We visualize a golden cord that connects your Higher Self to your physical body, entering the seat of consciousness (the head) and anchoring itself in the seat of emotion (the heart), where it glows with a triple flame of blue, gold and rose. That flame is invisible even to you until it is awakened when you call upon your Inner Christ. With repeated treatments, your Higher and Lower Selves move closer together until they become the single being they truly are, as in the integration of a "multiple personality." Your physical self, your Higher Self and the Inner Christ are three aspects of the whole "I AM, the eternal Trinity, represented by the triple flame.

The Mighty "I AM" Presence

The Causal Body

The colors of the Causal Body (Aura) are, in order, from the head outward: Blue, Yellow (or Golden Yellow), Rose, White, Green, Golden-Ruby (analogous to, but never referred to as Orange) and Violet. The colors of the spheres, these Rays, represent the macrocosm, the greater universe; their presence around the individual signifies his existence as a microcosm or lesser universe. Each symbolizes the virtues that you can, with study and practice, learn to radiate for the benefit of others.

The virtues are represented as follows:[4]

1 - Blue: Representative of the Will of God, His will as an inherent virtue in you; Power, Faith, Goodness, Happiness, Peace and Equilibrium (Harmony).

2 - Golden Yellow: Representative of the second person in the Trinity, Intelligence, Wisdom, Light, Understanding, Peace.

3 - Rose: Divine love, Adoration, Opulence, Beauty, Peace.

4 - White: Representing Purity, Art, Peace; achieves the Resurrection and the Ascension.

5 - Green: Truth, Health, Sanction (Moral Judgment), Music, Consecration, Concentration, Peace.

6 - Golden-Ruby: Grace, Providence, Sustenance, Peace.

7 - Violet: Forgiveness, Mercy, Transmutation, Peace.

---

4 Notice that all the Rays disseminate Peace.

Once you have learned these Rays and their characteristics thoroughly, you will be able to invoke their ruling Entities, and ask them to surround with their light anyone upon whom you wish goodness and peace. The following will familiarize you with those Entities.

The Governors of the Cosmos

By the Law of Correspondence, the Higher Planes have their own hierarchy of rulers—though "government" at this level is free of corruption, muddle-headedness, self-service, vote-seeking and compromise. (In short, it is free of politics.) Those who rule the Seven Spheres are instruments of God, ascended human beings and angels. Some are historical figures, some are known to us only by legend.

In the words of Saint-Germain: "The activities of the Great White Brotherhood are so diverse and widespread that hundreds and hundreds of ascended beings are needed to direct and govern the multiple lines of force that insure the progress of the human race." In other words, this is a job beyond the capabilities of one individual, however highly evolved.

And evolution, that of all the souls which exist, is the goal of the Great White Brotherhood, established by the Master Sanat Kumara many centuries ago. In that time, the consciousness of many children of this planet have been elevated to such heights that some became Lords of the Flame—the Masters who would in turn teach others to project their own light. God wants His children to know the joy of creation, and the different worlds (or planes) were created to allow men and women to experiment with the creative forces. Even on earth, the power of "I AM," the art of polarization, the force of the spoken word in various treatments (scientific prayer) allow us to create the conditions under which we live.

The Directors of the Rays: Masters of Wisdom

I've already mentioned that the Lords of the Rays have among their number some who have been described as mythical beings. But remember, all myth and legend is a body of tales built around a core of fact. (We know George Washington existed—and that the cherry tree was an invention of a writer of history for children, set down to illustrate the character of a great leader.) If you find some of the following difficult to accept, don't worry about it. Just read on; belief will come as you need it.

Each Ray is governed by an Ascended Master, an Archangel (of the hierarchy of angelic evolution), and an Elohim (of the hierarchy of elemental evolution), as well as a host of other entities we call angels. (Elohim is one of the Hebrew words for God; it is the plural of Eloh, god. This gives rise to some confusion, Biblically, since the translation of Genesis might read: "In the beginning the gods created..." In the plural, it is usually understood to mean "God of gods"; however, the Elohim are the gods of the elemental kingdom and are creators in their own right. If they directed the birth of this planet out of the young sun's leftovers, it was according to God's blueprints.)

The Blue Ray

The Blue Ray is the First Ray, and is governed by the Ascended Master El Morya.

This Master's origins are obscure, possibly extraterrestrial. His earthly incarnations are Arthur Pendragon (the "legendary" King Arthur of Camelot), Sir Thomas More, statistician and humanist of the 11th and 12th centuries, St. Thomas Moore, canonized Irish poet and writer of the 18th century and the Shah Jehan, builder of the Taj Mahal.

(Those who have seen him say that he maintains the appearance of this last incarnation.)

The Archangel of the Blue Ray is Michael. His mission is serving those who die on earth; he is a warrior angel, and his symbolic sword cuts the bonds that tie those who die with a heavy load of error and negative actions of their consciences from the darkness that would hold them. It is Michael whom we should invoke to free the souls of loved ones so they may move to the next life.

The Elohim of the Blue Ray is Hercules and his complement Amazonas. (We all have our complements; they are formed at the first (spiritual) cellular division, at which time both cells continue dividing to become distinct entities. Both souls are drawn to each other by bonds of love and often meet in successive lifetimes, until their incarnations are ended and they are united for eternity. The phrase, "Whom God hath joined together, let no man put asunder," refers to such perfect unions, and not properly to the earthly marriage.)

The Elohim are the highest of the Elemental beings, and rule over the Devas, the elemental builders of mountains and lakes, who are guardians over their creations, the seas, the communities, even the ancient trees of our planet.

In the celestial protocol, the rule is that "invocation commands an answer," and so, by calling on any of the entities of light—Masters, Archangels and Angels and Elohim—you command a response as swift and as powerful as your faith is strong.

The powerful Elohim Hercules answers immediately, surrounding you and anyone you may intercede for with his strength. And invocation to him, to the Master El Morya or to Michael the Archangel brings peace, power, happiness, equilibrium, goodness, and strength of will.

The Yellow Ray

The Yellow Ray is the second Ray, representing intelligence, the second person of the Eternal Trinity. This is the Ray of Wisdom, light and understanding. As the diagram at the end of this chapter illustrates, it brings the light of understanding, intellectual mastery and mental strength to all who seek these qualities.

Until very recently, the Lord of the Yellow Ray was Ascended Master Kuthumi; however, his evolution elevated him to the position of World Instructor, together with Ascended Master Jesus, and his rule of the Yellow Ray passed to Ascended Master Lanto. (Kuthumi had many incarnations, among them Pythagoras, the Magus Melchior, St. Francis of Asissi and St. Martin de Porres. Together with Master Morya, he guided the foundation of the school of Theosophy, through the medium of Madame Elena Petrovna Blavatski.)

The Archangel of the Golden Ray is Jofiel. The Elohim is Cassiopeia. To invoke this Ray, and the Wisdom it brings, mentalize (visualize) yourself wrapped in a brilliant yet soft golden-yellow light, like a luminous, weightless robe of golden silk. Do this as you fall asleep and experience waking up with a sense of peace and understanding.

The Rose Ray

The Rose Ray, Channel of the Holy Spirit, is the third Ray, the Ray of the Divine Love, and is ruled by the Ascended Mistress Mme. Rowena. (Her predecessor was the Ascended Master Paul the Venetian, who was also the painter Pablo el Veronés, whose paintings are on view in the Chateau de Liberté in Marseilles.) Little is known about Mme. Rowena, except that in her lifetime on earth she was considered one of the most beautiful women in the world, and that she was the historical model for Rowena in Sir Walter Scott's Ivanhoe. Her complement is

Victor, who is to be invoked whenever you wish to triumph in any endeavor.

The Archangel of the Rose Ray is called Chamuel, and his complement is Charity (Caridad). You should invoke Chamuel whenever you are in need of money or things are in need of repair. Bless the material things you have, your job, your bank account, your bills, your wallet; and bless all those mechanical objects you possess which are not working properly. Surround each of these with a vision of the Rose Flame and its Angels. You will witness small miracles.

The Elohim of the Rose Flame is Orion, the hunter, whose constellation is visible in the Northern Hemisphere. His complement is Angelica.

The Rose Ray is magnetic, attractive. Whenever you wish to attract someone or something, mentally fill the void that separates your from your desire with Rose Light, and let it surround that person or object. Your will be mutually attracted in perfect Harmony.

The White Ray

The White Ray, is the Fourth Ray, dividing the primary from the secondary colors with its purity. It is the totality of all colors.

The Lord of the White Ray is the Ascended Master Serapis Bey, who was first among the seraphim who came to earth as guardians of the first human being. He has controlled the White Flame since first saved it from the destruction of Atlantis by bringing it to Egypt.

The Archangel of the White Ray is Gabriel, the annunciator. The Elohim of the White Ray is called Beloved Clarity, Known as the Purifier. He is invoked to brighten the life and light in every atom and to banish the darkness. The angels of the White Flame are called the Brotherhood of Luxor.

The Green Ray

The Green Ray is the Fifth Ray, that of Truth, concentration and consecration.

The Lord of the Green Ray is the Ascended Master Hilarion, who was St. Paul in his Christian incarnation.

The Archangel of the Fifth Ray is Raphael, known as "the Heavenly Physician." The Elohim is Cyclopea or Vision, representative of the all-seeing Eye of God. He is also the Elohim of music.

You should invoke the Angels of the Green Ray when confronted with illness. Visualize all that illness or untruth as being wrapped in the lambent green mantle of Truth and the false will become true, the hidden will emerge into the open.

"Marie Celeste," the mother of Jesus, acts under the Green Ray to bring protection to all women about to give birth and all children about to be born. Ask that any mother-to-be and her unborn child be placed under her protection and ask that they be given to the Violet Ray, which will transmute their karma to the positive pole.

The Gold-Ruby Ray

The Gold-Ruby Ray, the Sixth Ray, is the Ray under which Jesus Christ acted to bring peace, healing and God's grace to mankind. Its Lord is the Ascended Mistress Nada, also known as the Patroness of Understanding.

The Archangel of the Sixth Ray is Uriel and the Elohim is Tranquilino, or Serenity. This is the Ray of Peace and Providence (sustenance). It is to be applied whenever you feel nervous or agitated, when a situation needs a peaceful resolution or when you are in need; this is best done just before going to sleep.

The Violet Ray

The Violet Ray, the Seventh Ray, brings the transmutation of karma, forgiveness and mercy.

Its Lord is the Ascended Master Saint-Germain, who has had many incarnations. Among them: St. Joseph, Saint Alban (the British martyr), the Doctor-Monk Roger Bacon of the 13th Century, Christian Rosenkreutz (founder of the Rosicrucians in the 14th Century), Hunyadi Janos (liberator of Hungary, 15th Century), Proclus (the great Neoplatonist of the 16th Century), Sir Francis Bacon (Lord Verulam, 17th Century) and lastly Prince Rakoczy, le Comte Saint-Germain (last of the Royal House of Transylvania, who lived during the French Revolution—a mysterious figure who engineered the escape of many good people condemned to the guillotine, who helped place Catherine the Great on her rightful throne and who, three years after his death at the end of the 18th Century, appeared to friends and students in Paris.)

Master Saint-Germain is the Avatar of the New Era, who will act through evolved people here on Earth to prepare us mentally for this Era of Truth. The Violet Ray liberates us from the bonds of negative karma through its powers of forgiveness and transmutation, and should be invoked by all who wish the understanding that will guide them to the positive pole. It is not God's way to condemn a person for his acts, and the Violet Flame is the light that leads us out of the darkness of error.

The Archangel of the Violet Ray is Sadkiel. Its Elohim is Acrturus.

The 7 Rays and their Components

(table)

Ray	Color	Virtue	Influence	Attraction	Characteristics in the Unevolved	Director	Archangel	Elohim
1°	Blue	Faith, Peace, Happiness, Balance, Will	Power, Initiative, Protection, Strength	Executives, Statesmen	Stubbornness, Aggressiveness, Wish to dominate	Ascended Master El Morya	Michael	Hercules (Amazons)
2°	Yellow	Intelligence, Illumination, Wisdom	Wisdom, Mental Strength, Intuition	Teachers, Students	Intellectual Pride, Knowledge at the expense of Innocence	Ascended Master Lanto	Jofiel	Cassiopeia
3°	Rose	Pure Love, Beauty, Opulence, Cohesion	Divine Love, Tolerance, Adoration	Arbiters, Pacifiers	Carnal Love, Indiscriminate Sexuality	Ascended Mistress Lady Rowena	Chamuel (Caridad Charity)	Orion (Angelica)
4°	White	Ascension, Purity, Resurrection	The Arts (Music, Graphics)	Artists, Dancers, Musicians	Artistic Pretension, Undisciplined Living	Ascended Master Serapis Bey (of the Devic Evolution)	Gabriel	Charity
5°	Green	Truth, Healing, Consecration, Concentration	Sciences, (Music as science)	Doctors, Inventors, Composers	Atheism, Faithlessness	Ascended Master Hilarion	Raphael	Cyclopea (Vision)
6°	Gold and Ruby	Peace, Grace, Sustenance	Devotional Orders, Serenity, Patience	Priests, Healers	Religious Fanaticism, Snobbery	Ascended Master Nada	Uriel	Tranquilino (Serenity)
7°	Violet	Compassion, Transmutation, Mercy, Liberation, Forgiveness	Culture, Refinement, Diplomacy, Prudence	Diplomats, Mystics Cultural Leaders	Vanity, Pride, Airs of	Ascended Master Saint-Germain	Sadkiel	Arcturus

A Few Words about the Elemental World

There are worlds which are invisible to us at this stage in our evolution as individuals and as a race. Jesus spoke of death as "the last enemy to conquer"; he referred to the fact that life is unending, and that "death" is the event that separates those of us who remain behind from our loved ones, and all who have passed before us. When death is conquered, it will be because we have evolved to the point where we can see beyond that barrier, and share the continued life of those we knew and loved, and the billions who precede and will follow them. This time will become the unification of all worlds.

One of these is the Elemental World, which is inhabited by beings similar to but unlike ourselves. They are the beings which gave rise to such myths and legends as elves, dryads, gnomes in mythology and children's tales. It is no wonder that Christ said, "Suffer the little children to come unto me, for theirs is the kingdom of Heaven." He also said, "Blessed are the poor in spirit, for theirs is the kingdom of Heaven. Blessed are the pure in heart, for they shall see God." These are references to the child in all of us. "Poor in spirit" means "innocent," unburdened by the sophistication of the modern world that renders us unable to maintain the pure, unquestioning acceptance of children. A wealth of knowledge limits us, for it closes our minds to those things we "know" cannot be. When Jesus said it was easier for a "camel to pass through the eye of a needle" than for a rich man to enter the Kingdom of Heaven. He referred not only to the greed and pride that are so often characteristic of wealth, but to that "wealth" of intellect that cripples belief and faith. There are worlds unseen to us and to deny ourselves the opportunity to see them someday—to abandon innocence—is true poverty. In perfect Harmony, innocence can exist side by side with knowledge, each adding to the other.

The Seventh Race

You have now read and, I hope, studied all three of the instructional books in this series, and in arriving at this point, you have in hand all the instruction I can give you. From here on, it is up to you. (But by now you know that there is much more to "you" than you ever thought!) If you practice all you have learned sincerely and faithfully, if your belief has reached the point of faith—of knowing the truth that is yours to wield—you will become one of the anointed, the chosen, who have freed themselves from the strictures of physical laws. You will have achieved a State of Grace.

You will no longer have to fight for the gains you wish to make in life, for your voice, your words, your Self will carry a wand of Truth. With only a mental decree, the Father's will come to you, and you will need to seek no further communications or messages from outside sources: The "still, small voice of calm" that speaks within you—your Higher Self—will guide you along your proper path, without doubt or error.

To help you to grow in the knowledge of the Flames, we have developed a small pamphlet entitled Daily Meditations, published by an Organization called Bridge to Freedom directed by the Master El Morya under the pseudonym of Thomas Printz. It is available in both and English Spanish at a nominal price through the publishers of these volumes.

As the strength of the Rays grows within you, you will gradually become a candidate for Ascension, the most desirable of Earthly states, since it indicates that you have been cleansed of all negative karmas from previous lives, and have arrived at the end of a long journey of incarnations. It indicates that you have manifested within yourself your own Divine Plan, the purpose for which you were created and have lived so many lifetimes to achieve. The time of the New World is near, that time which Jesus predicted: "The Hour of Salvation and the Time of Acceptance."

During the year 1969, a thousand children of the Seventh Race were born, children of highly evolved enlightenment, mature, cultured, patient and uniquely courteous almost from birth. They are a "race" of geniuses, scientists, clairvoyants who are beginning to come of age. They will soon show their superiority, as they begin to take control of governments, corporations, the major organizations of mankind. You will know them as they establish themselves in the public eye by their serenity and wisdom.

The clash of the new order against the old is more evident today than ever, and we must consider that not all of today's "rebellious" youth are delinquents and social misfits. Many are speaking up for your freedoms just as much as for their own. Those who would keep pace with the new age would be well advised to study psychology and metaphysics. Without the knowledge this learning will bring, they will be left behind as the world enters into its New Age.

Suggested Invocations

*I*n the next few pages, I offer some appropriate invocations for activating the Violet and other Flames for specific and general purposes. These are guidelines, given for form and content, and I am sure you will soon want to develop invocations of your own, in language you will be more comfortable with. In the meantime, I am sure you will find the following invocations valuable and effective.

Invocation for protection, to be repeated daily in order to create and maintain the impetus that will keep it in force:

I AM the victorious Presence of the Almighty, and I cover myself with my robe of purest, most brilliant light, which renders me invisible and invincible in the face of all wrongs and all human creation for all time.

Another protective invocation, also said daily:

I AM the victorious Presence of God and I AM surrounded by my Violet Fire. I AM lit throughout my Being wherever I may be in the world. All my human creations are changed by my Flame… all energy I have used badly against all elements, all animals, all men, women and children, all creatures, all life… all wrong thoughts, negative, destructive or impure in nature… all design, pattern or habit of hate, jealousy, ill-will, disagreeableness, maledictions, lies, vindictiveness or anger. Let all these be transmuted. (Repeat this last sentence three times.) Let all effects, records or memories of them be changed before they can be materialized, manifested or begun. Let all these be transmuted so that I may find myself in a pure state of harmony.

An invocation to be used whenever we find ourselves dwelling on some negative, destructive or self-defeating thought:

I AM the Law of Pardon and the Transmuting Flame for all errors or transgressions I may have committed. I AM the Transmuting Flame for all errors committed by all humankind. I AM lit by Violet Fire, which is outside the realm of all human creation, and which is now and forever maintained.

To be used in times of self-doubt:

Most beloved Presence of God in me, I affirm and declare in Your name: I AM the Resurrection and the Life of God's Glory, the Wisdom and the Power contained in my Etheric Body before the world began. All inferior traces within me are now and herewith dissolved by the Power of the Sacred Flame.

To be used against all types of manifestation which may be bothering us at any time:

I close the Astral Doorway, my aura and the aura of my home. I invoke the Angels of the Rose Flame to come and fill me and to surround this manifestation, and I ask the same for all who live on our planet.

A brief exorcism to banish any entity that may bother us or try to inhabit our earthly bodies or those of others:

In the name of the most beloved Presence of God, the I AM in me, I invoke you, (name, if known), and tell you that I love you, I love you, I love you. Now, in the name of Love, RETURN TO THE FATHER and take care of His matters in your world as I do in mine. So be it!

A protective invocation for those who are able to depart at will from the Terrestrial Plane:

In the name of the most beloved Presence of God in me, I AM, I now invoke the beloved Archangel Michael to come to my aid and to the aid of all men, women and children who may depart their bodies in this 24-hour period. Instantly cut the ties of magnetism and gravity that seek to hold us to this Earth and to Earthly appetites and passions. Send your Angelic armies to surround us and guide us beyond the Earth's atmosphere and influence to a plane of light and peace. Prepare us for our appearance before the white-robed Karmic Tribunal. Accept the Good inside our Causal Bodies as an offering before this Council of Judgment, that all souls may be carried to the Centers of Learning, where we may best learn the Law, so that we may reincarnate, if necessary, in Harmony, better equipped to win our individual battle in thy Light. Thank you, most beloved Prince of the Angelic Hosts, for your Presence among us and for your constant care and protection at the time of our passing and in all our days.

For those in darkness, torment and error:

Beloved Presence of God, the I AM in me and in them, in the name of the beloved Master Jesus Christ, I invoke all Angels and entities of the Blue Flame. Father, forgive them, for they know not what they do. Sever the ties that bind those who are in darkness and have none to intercede for them. Beloved Prince Michael, take them to higher planes of study, peace and light. I thank you for your loving aid.

For those on their deathbeds:

Beloved Presence of God, the I AM in me, I bow before whatever destiny is necessary for my brother (sister), and ask the Consoling Saint to surround his (her) soul with peace and with the souls of his (her) loved ones. Let them manifest themselves in these last moments on the planet in peace, harmony, purity and joy. Let him (her) quickly and gently pass from his (her) physical temple to the kingdom of the Spirit.

For those about to be born:

Beloved Presence of God in me and in these children, beloved Archangel Gabriel, light the Flame of Resurrection in, around and over those who await the moment of incarnation, so that they may bring to this new life all the glory and goodness of the Christ within them. So let it be!

To invoke the power of God's will, through the entity called Crystal; to be said daily:

Beloved Crystal, reverently I invoke you to offer you the cleansing of all my past incarnations, from the beginning of time until today. Purify all my earthly vessels and all my world, including all energies I may use or have used, and let your powers make me responsible in dealing with the lives and behavior of others.

For protection of the home against wrongdoers and other entities, earthly or otherwise:

Angels of the Rose Flame (said three times), come (three times) light (three times) the Rose Flame of Divine Love around my home, its windows and doors, and cover my loved ones and neighbors with your Light; let all that comes in contact with the boundaries of this Force feel the strength of Divine Love and lose all desire to do harm to others or their property. In love I ask it.

To protect against bad intentions, injury or damage by a third party, and to bring Goodness to all who ask it:

Beloved Presence of God in me and in (person's name), I beseech the Christ in (name) to talk directly to him (her). I remind you that you are the perfect child of God, generous, noble, just and honest. I greet you and remind you that you do not want your Lower Self to behave in any way that may be contrary to the Immaculate Concept and to your personal Harmony. I thank you because I know that you hear and understand, and that your temple is already being put in order.

To unmask and counteract lies or resentments in us or in others:

In the name of the beloved Presence of God in me (in name), I now cover this situation with the cloak of Truth and the light of the Green Flame, and I ask to see this Truth. Thank you, Father, for I know you have heard me.

In all situations presenting disharmony:

I bless the Good in this situation, and I ask to see it demonstrated. Thank you, Father, for I know you have heard me.

* * *

May these and your own invocations, prayers and treatments bring happiness and perfect harmony to your life!

Book IV

Who is and Who was The Count Saint-Germain

Introduction

*I*n this brief volume, I have not attempted to offer a complete biography or the ultimate truth regarding the man known as Count Saint-Germain or the Ascended Master Saint-Germain, who are the same person. My purpose herein is first to explain as completely as possible with the facts and testimonies at our disposal some enigmas about the Count, particularly following his disappearance in the 18th century. Secondly, I will attempt to communicate certain revelations about Saint-Germain and his activities and purposes, which will become more understandable to you as you near the end of this book.

The explanations and revelations herein will also be valuable to you in your studies in the metaphysical teachings of the New Era, much of which has been communicated to us by the Master Saint-Germain.

At the end of the book, you will find a comprehensive bibliography of writings about this enigmatic man. However, I recommend a certain amount of caution in accepting much of what has been written about him; so much was written at times of spiritual ignorance, by people who were themselves far from expert at separating fact from fancy—sensationalist reporters, biographers and memoirists who allowed preconceptions, conjectures and personal opinions to color what they set down as fact.

From medieval times through the 18th century, a majority of Europe's secular and religious leaders were stumbling blocks in the path of man's spiritual growth. Indeed, until recently, a majority of the great metaphysical truths have been debunked or ignored; but today, more and more people are discovering the Law of Mentalism and the power of the Violet Flame, and human consciousness has begun to ascend the great Ladder of Initiation, approaching a new age of understanding and taking those first steps toward the I AM Presence— toward the God that is within us all.

CONNY MÉNDEZ

Part I

The Historic Saint-Germain

Le Comte de Saint-Germain

*L*iterally volumes have been written about the mysterious Count Saint-Germain, the "Man of Marvels" who was so prominent on the European scene during the turbulent 18th Century.

Official archives and Foreign Affairs records of the times throughout Europe contain numerous mentions of the Count, and alter his disappearance, his unique personality became the basis for some of the world's best-known fictional characters—among them: The Count of Monte Cristo by Alexandre Dumas (père), Zanoni by Bulwer-Lytton, The Scarlet Pimpernel by Baroness Orczy, and a series of recent fantasy novels by Chelsea Quinn Yarbro.

The Count was surrounded by two strong human currents. On the one hand, he was the object of envy, spite and jealousy because he commanded the respect and friendship of royalty, noted political, social and academic figures across the Continent. And, on the other hand, he was held in high esteem, almost awe, by alchemists, members of secret societies and students of the occult, as well as the leaders of society. The first group did its best to exile, jail or destroy him; he was accused of being a charlatan at best, a traitor at worst. But he was never found guilty of the slightest transgression, nor did he ever betray a trust. No one was ever able to determine the source of his

Le Comte de Saint-Germain

seemingly unlimited income; he never dealt with banks or bankers, nor was any of his wealth obtained from those with whom he came in contact. His credit was unquestioned, and never reached the breaking point. Several attempts were made to capture and imprison him on trumped-up charges—all unsuccessful: He simply vanished from the public eye, only to turn up almost immediately in another country or city, as urbane and unruffled as ever.

None of the existing writings about the Count truly explain the enigmas and mysteries surrounding him; they are all based on conjectures, suppositions and opinions. Here was a man who spoke of having lived for thousands of years, who would take a small gem from a friend and return one of the same cut and character, saying that he had "grown" it by alchemical means, a man who was never seen to eat or drink by any who knew him, a man of measureless wealth, of distinct musical talent and other unique abilities (he was well known for being able to write with both hands simultaneously, and his signature was the same with either hand). But nothing written about him seeks to explain these characteristics through any but the most frivolous speculation. Drawing on metaphysical or spiritual awareness allows us to reach the conclusion that he was an enlightened presence—an Adept or special messenger from the White Hierarchy, sent to fulfill multiple missions with a myriad of obligations.

History tells us that he was born May 26, 1696, the youngest son of Prince Franz Leopold Rakoczy (Ferenc II) and Princess Charlotte Amadea de Hesse Rheinfels of Transylvania.

Dethroned and persecuted by Charles VI, Ferenc II wished to protect his son from political enemies, and circulated false news of the boy's early death, and smuggled him to the family manor in Florence, where he was educated by Gian-Gastone de Medici. The young prince showed early signs of intelligence and high spiritual development; by the age of 14, he was already influential in the French-Italian Masonic movement, and was continuing his studies at the University of Siena.

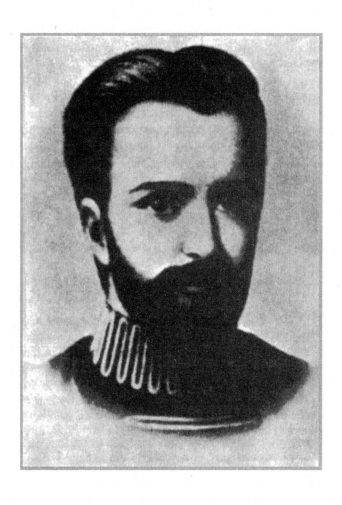

Prince Rakoczy

In the meantime, Austro-Hungarian politics exerted their pressure:
The Prince's father, Ferenc II, a patriot who was considered far too
popular with the people for the well-being of those in power, was
exiled to Turkey, where he lived with his small entourage until his
death in 1735. The prince, then 39, came to his father's deathbed, and
after Ferenc's passing undertook a diplomatic mission on behalf of
the Sultan which took him home again to Transylvania. Ironically, his
"early" demise was once again recorded in that same year, possibly in
confusion with his father, since they shared the same name. (Ferenc in
Magyar, Franz in German, or Franciscus in its Latinate form.)

Little is known of the Prince during the following years.
Nationalistic Hungarian historians referred to him as "the son of a
German mother, who never lived in Hungary, who grew up far from
the Rakoczy tradition, an alien in his own land." His history, as we can
glean it from existing records and references, is a mass of contradictions
and accusations.

At the time of his father's death, the people of Hungary were on
the verge of declaring him their leader—and at the same time, various
rumors began to circulate. At the time of his father's death, he is "seen"
in Holland, conferring with the president of London's Royal Society,
a prominent Rosicrucian. At the time when he was with the Sultan
in Turkey, he is reported to be the guest of the Shah of Persia. At the
time of his "death" he was supposedly in Turkey and in Transylvania;
a matter of weeks later, he mysteriously reappears in Scotland, where
he lived in comparative obscurity until 1743. Over the years, he took
a number of names and nationalities, making rare appearances as the
Marquis de Montferrat, Count Bellamare, Herr Schoenig, Mr. Weldon,
M. de Surmont and Count Soltikoff. It was not until May of 1743 that
he arrived in Paris, where he lived quietly for a number of years, and
it was not until 1758 that he introduced himself to Marshall Belle Isle
as le Comte de Saint-Germain.

The Marshall presented the Count to Madame Pompadour, who introduced him to Louis XV. It is from this point on that most of what we know of Rakoczy as the Count is recorded.

Through he is said to have told Louis secretly of his identity, he never used the name Rakoczy after that time. His impact on this timeless city during this historic era was subtle, yet remarkable.

* * *

Chronologically, Prince Rakoczy must have been 62 when he met Marshall Belle Isle, yet his appearance was that of a man at least 20 years younger—and he was described as looking just as young in 1786 (the year of his historic "death"), some 28 years later, when he would have been 90.

All sources describe the Count as a youthful gentleman of noble bearing and dignity, of impeccable refinement and courtesy. He had small, strong hands and small feet, dark hair and intense brown eyes. (One of his biographers, Countess d'Adhemar, repeated over and over "What eyes! I have never seen eyes like his!")

His manners and bearing bore out his noble lineage. He was a sober dresser, almost invariably dressed in black, and in the finest of materials; the only flashes of color in his clothing came from the jewels he wore.

Judging by the magnificence of those jewels, he was considered a man of immense wealth. He wore splendid buttons, cufflinks, watches and chains. He often displayed an enormous opal and an extraordinary white sapphire the size of an egg. The variety, size and perfection of his diamonds attracted great attention.

He was said to have two footmen and four servants, uniformed in dark brown livery trimmed with gold braid. His endless knowledge on a diversity of subjects, his wit and musical abilities made him a welcome guest at parties and banquets in the finest residences, yet no one could claim to have visited him at his own home, Hotel Transylvania (so named for his father's years of residence there from 1713 to 1717). He was most secretive about his private life, though when others commented on his remarkably youthful appearance, he would often make the claim that he had discovered (or concocted) a marvelous elixir that had kept him alive for two thousand years—a remark that occasioned considerable speculation on who was the patriarch and who the scion of the noble Rakoczy line.

Saint-Germain was, by every account, a polished diplomat, a talented and accomplished artist and a composer and musician of virtuoso ability. It is said that his painting and sculpture were on a par with the masters of his day. His piano technique was renowned, and his abilities on the violin foreshadowed the artistry of Paganini. (Unfortunately, only one of his compositions remains in its entirety, an aria from his opera "L'Incostanza Delusa," composed in the light and flowery manner of the 18th century.

Why did the Prince choose the name Saint-Germain? There had long been links between the Rakoczy name and Saint-Germain. The family holdings in Italy were said to be "of Saint-Germain." And the Prince's (and his father's) residence in Paris still stands today at 9 Quai Malaquais in le Faubourg Saint-Germain. It seems a logical choice of names for his identity at this period in his life.

There is a masonic connection as well: The Latin phrase comes sancti germanici ("companion of the holy fellowship") is a familiar one to the Masons of France. Saint-Germain was a founding member of French Masonry (indeed, he proclaimed himself "the oldest of all Masons") and the name he chose was singularly appropriate, to his venue and to his mission in behalf of humanity as a member of the White Brotherhood.

Nearly a century after the "death" of Saint-Germain, The Theosophical Society announced the following message, delivered by an Adept of the White Brotherhood known only as "The Tibetan":

"The Master specifically in charge of fixture human development throughout Europe, and of the mental awareness throughout America is Master Rakoczy. He is Hungarian and resides in the Carpathian Mountains, and was at one time a prominent member of the Hungarian court. He also had a great following when he was known as the Count Saint-Germain. In the lodge of the White Fraternity, he is usually referred to as 'The Count', and in America, he functions as the general administrator of the highest planes of the Brotherhood. It may be said that he is responsible for the carrying out of Christ's master plans in the physical plane."

The message is clear. "Mental awareness in America" refers to the principles of Mentalism, given us by Hermes Trismegistus and given nationwide emphasis by Mary Baker Eddy, the founder of Christian Science, who was a leading proponent of the coming Era of the Woman as well as a leading spokesman for the Mental Principle.

The message also speaks of Master Rakoczy in the present tense, saying that he is in charge of European and American awareness, that he resides in the Carpathians. It states that Saint-Germain is carrying out the works of Christ for the present era, in other words manifesting himself as the Christ of this age.

How does an Adept or Master manifest himself? For brief periods, it is only necessary for him or her to increase the density of the etheric body to the point of visibility. For longer periods of time, a Master may occupy a "borrowed" body, which required considerably less expense of energy. The borrowed body is, of course, a willing lender, one who has been initiated into the Principles and who is willing to give up his body to act as a host to the soul or personality of the Master, either for a period during life or upon death.

Such a body must be in the best of health, and its original occupant highly evolved for it to fare well under the intense energies of a master's occupancy. The "transplant" is a gradual one, a period of acclimation.

The Adept who occupies the body has the power to reform and modify the physical structure in order to adapt it to his own needs. An example of this adaptation is Saint-Germain's ability to partake of spiritual Universal Sustenance—explaining why the Count had no need to eat or drink. (The Count, by his own admission, has occupied some forty "borrowed" bodies on various occasions and for various purposes or missions on this planet. One of these was that of St. Joseph, husband of the mother of Jesus; another is believed to be that of Christopher Columbus; and a third that of liberator Simón Bolívar.)

For a Master to appear on earth by means of reincarnation is impractical for any purpose of temporary or Immediate urgency; consider the fact that the reincarnated soul is born with no memory of this previous existence (or purpose), and that it must wait a minimum number of years to reach effective maturity in order to fulfill its mission. A temporary visual appearance or the borrowing of a willing host are more logical approaches.

* * *

One of the most remarkable of Count Saint-Germain's recorded abilities was his extraordinary memory. He could repeat verbatim page after page after a cursory scan of the material. He spoke flawless German, English, French, Italian, Spanish, Portuguese, Arabic, Chinese, and other oriental languages, Latin, Greek, Hebrew, Chaldean, Assyrian and Sanskrit, and could read the cuneiform writing of Babylon and Egyptian hieroglyphics with complete mastery.

The Count was also ambidextrous, and could write with both hands at the same time. The hemispheres of his brain were independent, allowing him to compose a sonnet with one hand and a letter to his bankers with the other.

Although he never boasted of his occult powers, records of his exploits tell us that he would spontaneously demonstrate his talents in the areas of White Magic and alchemy, as well as his knowledge as a Cabalist, Hermetist, FrancMason, Templar, Gnostic, Rosicrucian and Enlightened Being.

He was clairvoyant and clairaudient and could travel astrally, etherically and cosmically. He was known to disappear for days at a time. He could go into a deep, unwakable trance at any time... at his home or another's. The Viennese historian Franz Graeffner relates that in the middle of a conversation, the Count's lively and expressive eyes became colorless and blank, his body stiffened and remained rigid for several minutes. When he recovered, he stood up, made a farewell gesture with his hand and said, in German, "Ich scheide." (I'm leaving). "You will see me again tomorrow. In the meantime, I am needed in Constantinople and then in England. I must work on two inventions which will become known in the next century—a ship and a train."

The King, too, was aware of his powers, as the Count had the disconcerting habit of entering the Royal Chamber without bothering to use doors; he would simply appear and disappear without hiding his abilities.

At parties, he would entertain the company by relating in detail his friendship with Cleopatra, Jesus, the Queen of Sheba and Saint Isabel, his presence at Valois (the Royal Court of France from the 14th to the 16th Centuries), conversations with Saint Anne, facts relating to ancient Rome, Russia, Turkey, Austria, China, Japan and India. He could imitate Francis I, 16th Century King of France, reveal intimate details of the court of Louis XIV, and spoke of it all with the same casual manner one would use to discuss current events.

On one occasion, he paused in the middle of an episode from times long past and asked his valet. "Wasn't that the way it was, Roger?" Roger answered, "Milord forgets that I have only been with him these past four hundred years. That must have happened when my predecessor was in your employ." (This brings up a few interesting questions about the redoubtable Roger—which must remain unanswered, since almost nothing is known of the man. And what of Rakoczy's birth in Transylvania, less than half a century before? Had the Count and Roger been man and manservant in a previous incarnation? Or were they both occupying "borrowed" bodies at this time?)

Naturally, the Count's many mysterious abilities were classified under the heading of "magic" by the standards of his day (not to mention our own time). But as metaphysicians, we know that all things have a perfectly natural explanation, that all powers and abilities are ours by inheritance from our Divine Creator.

When a human being reaches his or her last incarnation on Earth, it is said that he or she is a candidate for Ascension. Ascension occurs when a person has shed all ties to this planet, to all earthly relatives, all negative energies have been canceled, and his or her cells have begun to fill with light. At this time, Earth's physical and spiritual gravity has been conquered; the Higher Self "I AM" exerts its force to pull the person away from Earth. It is at this moment that the person has the choice of eternal Glory or continuing to aid humanity in its quest for enlightenment. At the same time, the subconscious empties itself into the conscious, and the individual remembers all past incarnations, experiences and knowledge with no pain or suffering whatsoever. All abilities, languages and enlightenment acquired in all past lives are restored to the person, and all the "Treasures of Heaven"—all that is encompassed by the person's Causative Body—are at his or her disposal. These special abilities are retained if the individual chooses to continue serving humanity, discarded as unnecessary if the individual chooses his or her well-earned spiritual reward.

The talents of those who continue to aid humanity in the Ascended state, therefore, are simply the accumulation of many lifetimes' abilities. Ambidexterity is the recollection of lives as both a right-handed and a left-handed person. An extraordinary memory is a natural ability released from past lives, the ability to read the past, free of the veil of Maya (Illusion), the ability to recall information seen at a glance without the limitations of a brain that is 90 percent unused. The "magical" practice of appearing and disappearing at will, without resorting to the mundanity of doors is an ability of the astral and etheric bodies available to the occupant of a "borrowed" body. This ability is achieved through study and practice, over several lifetimes. In our own physical lives, we "leave" our bodies and "travel" while asleep—a hint of the talents that will someday be ours.

* * *

The source of Count Saint-Germain's enormous wealth was a constant subject of speculation and gossip throughout Paris. His seemingly unlimited credit, opulent jewels, elegant clothing and sumptuous lifestyle naturally attracted attention, and the resultant speculation ended in the conclusion that his skull as an alchemist had made him rich beyond the dreams of even the nobility of his day.

It was as good an explanation as any. The Law of Correspondence— "As it is above, so it is below; as it is below, so it is above"—tells us that alchemy exists in correspondent forms on all planes. Its practice is easier as one ascends through the spiritual planes, and alchemical transformations are most difficult on the material earthly plane.

The transmutation of base metal into gold is analogous to the transformation of energy in the Mental/Spiritual plane. It is a matter of turning all negative forms and mental images into the "golden" virtues that are ours by right on the "I AM" plane—by recognizing and affirming the perfection that is the only Truth.

Cicero said that philosophy is the knowledge of divine and human characteristics and their causes, the principles by which they exist and operate. The "Philosopher's Stone," that elusive abstraction that was to alchemists what the Holy Grail was to medieval knights, was knowledge of how to transmute the elements. On the metaphysical level, it is that ultimate knowledge called Faith.

Alchemy is both spiritual and material. But one must learn the spiritual aspect first. Until one has learned to translate energy through the Violet Flame and later through the other Flames, he has yet to discover the "Philosopher's Stone." But once an alchemist has learned how to use the Flames, he can use that knowledge, that energy, that faith to perform the more earthly transmutations. (We are learning. We have been transmuting elements—even creating new and very short-lived elements not found on this planet—in nuclear experiments since the 1940s. But it is a slow and tedious process, since we have limited ourselves to the use of physical energies, rather than the spiritual.)

The alchemists of the past were generally very wise, well versed in the sciences and the occult practices of their times. They were also highly secretive, burying their formulas in the code of cabalistic signs and apparent gibberish. This was both to protect their hard-won knowledge and to protect the uninitiated from tampering with potentially dangerous substances and procedures.

Saint-Germain demonstrated his alchemical accomplishment on a few occasions. One of these was in the presence of Jacques Casanova de Seingalt. The count took a common copper coin, worth only a few centimes from Casanova, exposed it to a certain flame until it turned red, and when it had cooled sufficiently, returned it to him. The coin had turned to pure gold. Casanova found it hard to believe, and expressed his incredulity. Saint-Germain simply replied, "Whoever doubts my knowledge is not fit to speak to me," and showed his visitor to the door.

For an adept of the degree of the Count, all possibilities are facts. Transforming a common material such as copper into gold is a matter of extending one's hand, extracting molecules of gold from the surrounding environment and allowing them to supplant the copper molecules in the coin. There is only one formula for this process: The Law of Correspondence.

This is a truth that is virtually beyond comprehension or even belief for anyone who has not studied the Principle of Mentalism and made it an integral part of his consciousness. Because of this, the majority of alchemists continued to seek the secrets of transmutation the "easy" way, unaware of the simple truth. Some readers of this series of books will be at a level of achievement on the metaphysical scale that will allow them to visualize themselves surrounded by a Golden Flame descending from the Presence—and when that flame is truly felt and understood, it will allow them to reach forth and pluck from the air any substance they need. This is the spiritual Truth of Alchemy.

But there is a vital point that must be understood and adhered to; without it, spiritual alchemy cannot function. And that truth is that the I AM Presence, your Higher Self, cannot transmit its golden substance to the lower (earthly) self unless the channel is pure and unobstructed. This means that your earthly self must be free of bitterness and resentment—the emotional obstructions brought on by ill-will, vicious comments, vengeful actions, the constant remembrances of wrongdoings (yours or anyone else's) or any violent emotions. Forgiveness leads to equanimity, and equanimity clears the channel.

Achieving a constant state of equanimity requires making the effort never to be affected by any sad, anger-producing or other adverse emotional circumstances. Loss of patience, anger, irritation at your mistakes or those of others—the negative emotions in general—will affect your ability to receive the benefits of the good that your I AM Presence wishes to bestow on you. And, when you reach the higher levels of Spiritual Alchemy, any fluctuation in your feelings can destructively affect your environment, your family and friends, and, if you are a leader of a group, whether social or professional, it can affect all those who follow you. The simplest way to avert such dangers is to avoid, whenever possible, being present where dramatic, sad, or negative events are happening. Fortunately, a person who has reached this Octave, this stage of sensitivity, need not be present in order to help sick people. In fact, it is often better to declare your wish for their good health from a distance, since the Practitioner's personal vibrations are often too strong for the ailing person. The universal treatment of the sick one's Presence need not even be specific as to the problem: The Practitioner treats the whole "I AM", spiritual and physical. This is the true definition and intent of Holistic Medicine!

* * *

The Landgrave Charles de Hess-Cassel, Duke of Schleswig, was related to Prince Rakoczy on his mother's side (she was the Princess of Hesse Rheinfels). The Duke was an advanced occultist as well as a close friend of the Prince, and was perhaps the only person who knew the complete truth about le Comte de Saint-Germain.

If there was some doubt about Saint-Germain's birth in Transylvania, his alleged death at the Castle of Duke Charles In Eckernfoerde, Sweden on February 27, 1784 was even more unlikely. But this was not the first—nor the last—occasion upon which the Master would disappear, leaving neither body nor tomb to mark his passing… as we shall later see. Duke Charles burned all of the Count's papers following his disappearance, leaving intact only the manuscript of The Most Holy Trinosophy, at that time, the only book the Count had written.

Regarding the Count's death, Mme. Blavatsky commented over a century later in a Theosophical Society meeting: "Isn't it absurd that a man of the stature of Saint-Germain was buried without pomp or ceremony whatsoever, without official supervision, without the Police Registration which was always a must in the funerals of men of rank? Where were all these things? There's not even a paper to testify to it!"

Add to this valid question the fact the Count was reported to have been seen on numerous occasions after his supposed "demise" in a state conference with Queen Catherine of Russia in 1785; with Princess Lamballe moments before she went to the guillotine, and with Jeanne Dubarry, the King's paramour, also moments before her death, during the Reign of Terror in 1793. The Comte de Chalons also spoke of having a conversation with Saint-Germain at the San Marco Plaza the night before Chalons' departure for France in 1788. And even in this century, during the '20s, Bishop Leadbeater of the Liberal Catholic Church spoke of meeting Saint-Germain, dressed as any Italian gentleman of the day, in the Pincio, a plaza in Rome, where they spent at least an hour in conversation. There are many other such instances cited in the Saint-Germain Foundation books entitled Unveiled Mysteries and The Magic Presence; Included are his appearances, disappearances, periods of residency in various places, and conversations with various members of the Foundation as well as others.

Such reported appearances of the Count were frequent, but in recent years, there have been none. It is assumed that this is because he has ascended to a superior plane where his duties and responsibilities as Avatar of this era have occupied him elsewhere. However, the Master Maha Chohan has stated that the Master will soon require his physical form again, as those duties demand his presence in the physical plane.

Saint-Germain's greatest gift to us is the awareness of the Violet Flame and its powers and influences. This Flame is applied to egos about to ascend and is used in spiritual retreats. Its use is now part of metaphysical teachings.

Part II

A Man of Many Lives

The Lives of the Master Saint-Germain: His Reincarnations between the Years 303 and 1561 A.D.

Saint Albans. The first English martyr.
   Birth date unknown. Died 303 A.D.

Proclus. Greek philosopher. Neo-Platonist.
   Born 410, died 485 A.D.

Robertus. French Monk. Identity poorly documented.
   Lived approximately between 1110 and 1211 A.D.

Roger Bacon. The Medical Monk.
   Born 1214, died 1294 A.D.

Christian Rosencrantz. Founder of the Rosicrucian society.
   Born 1378, died 1484 A.D.

Francis Bacon. English Politician, Philosopher and Writer.
   Born in 1561 A.D., died 1626 A.D. Last known
   incarnation before his appearance as Prince Rakoczy/
   Saint-Germain. It is said that Bacon's tomb is empty.

A few Comments on the
Incarnations of Saint-Germain:

No incarnation of the Master as a woman has been recorded or surmised. Apparently, he was never married in any of his earthly lives.

Though Bishop C.W. Leadbeater of the Theosophical Society, in his book Masters and Their Paths, states that among Saint-Germain's many incarnations was the persona of Hunyadi Janos, the Defender of Hungary. I have chosen to exclude his name from this book (although I did mention Janos in a previous volume in this series). The reason is simply that there is an impossible overlap between Janos' life and that of the better-documented life of Rosenkreutz: Hungarian history states that Janos was born in 1386—8 years after the birth of Rosenkreutz— and that he died in 1459—25 years before Rosenkreutz' death. Since one soul cannot occupy two bodies simultaneously, I have left out the less likely of the two incarnations.

THE PUBLISHERS

The Ascended Master Saint-Germain

Preface

Orpheus of Thrace, poet and minstrel, seems to have been the originator of the great philosophical systems of the west.

From its beginnings as an unstructured and festive approach to religion in the Dionysian manner, Orphism embraced the many gods of Greece; however the true Orphics believed that the gods were not beings but symbols of divine principles, immutable laws or aspects of some Universal Mind. These are principles we know today as the Rays, the Flames, the Angelic Host, the White Hierarchy and all Cosmic Beings as facets of the Universal "I AM".

But symbolism becomes an irritant to the mind, a mental itch that must be scratched. Relief comes only with the search for and discovery of explanations. Greek intellectuals began to realize that their tradition of mythology was in fact a great puzzle, hiding vital spiritual truths, and they attacked this puzzle with all their abilities. The result was the awakening of the reasoning faculties and the stimulation of pure abstract thought. From this came the Golden Age of intense intellectual, practical and spiritual activity that was to produce in 300 years some 600 philosophers whose ideas forever changed the way mankind thought, dreamed and created.

During the same, period, in Egypt, the esoteric teachings, astrology and the study of geometry—then reserved only for the disciples of astrology—were growing at the same pace. It was students such as Pythagoras (who waited seven years to be accepted as a student of esoteric knowledge) who spread this mathematical knowledge to the western world. Plato, too, was an Orphic student who adapted many of the esoteric doctrines into his philosophy.

The Lives of the Master Saint-Germain

Saint Albans

*J*esus came into the world and spread the teachings that were to be known as Christianity (and which we call Christian metaphysics), thus opening the hermetic seal on Judaism of that time. The apostles and evangelists, following the instructions of Christ (after his ascension) spread these beliefs and principles, but it was an arduous task, measured by the spilling of Christian blood, and it was literally centuries before the new beliefs were accepted. Paul of Tarsus, Christianity's first missionary (and a medium, clairvoyant and clairaudient) was mainly responsible for giving Christ's teachings their greatest audience. Though he never met the Master Jesus, he heard His voice and experienced a manifestation from Him on the road to Damascus.

It was during the height of Christian martyrdom, when resistance to the growing influence of the new religion was at its bitterest, that Master Saint-Germain was reincarnated as an Anglo-Roman child in the city of Verulamium, located some twenty minutes from present-day London (Londinium) in what is now Herfordshire. The boy was Albano (or Albans)—born on the island that was to become the seat of the last and farthest spread of earth's empires—who would, as a Benedictine monk in his manhood, spread his powerful vibrations, and the teaching of Christianity, throughout the greatest empire of his day. His untiring efforts and spreading influence made him Christianity's loudest voice—and the first English martyr, in the year 303.

Sometime after his death, the Church and his devoted followers built an abbey on the site of his martyrdom and named it "Saint Albans." Centuries later, in 757, England was divided into small kingdoms. The king of one of these, Offa of Mercia, found the relics of Albans and built a Benedictine monastery in his honor; the monastery became one of the most important sites of the Benedictine order. Finally, in 1077, a great Gothic Cathedral was erected, using bricks from the ancient city of Verulamium.

Today, the 17th of June is celebrated throughout England as St. Albans Day.

Proclus

*I*n philosophical circles, it is said, with considerable justification, that the germ of any great idea today, including Christian ideas, can be found in the works of Plato.

While Christian ideology was gathering strength and followers, the beliefs which the church referred to as "Paganism"—Orphism and the Esoteric studies of which Plato was a principal proponent—were on the wane. It was a century after the death of Albans, during this time of ideological conflict, that Proclus was born in Byzantium.

Proclus studied in Alexandria, and was an avid follower of the philosopher Plotinus, who was also born in Alexandria some 200 years before Proclus, in about 205 A.D.

Plato's philosophy has been re-examined and reapplied to the quest for understanding of man's place in the universe a number of times—in the 14th century, as the Renaissance heralded man's struggle to emerge from the Dark Ages, and with the Cambridge School of the

Proclus, the Neo-Platonist

17th century—but it was Proclus who first revived Platonic thinking and applied it to his own era; thus, he was the first Neo-Platonist. As implied in the first paragraph of this section, Plato's thought continues to influence philosophers today. If you read Proclus, you will find that his Neo-Platonism is strikingly similar to modern metaphysics; it is the hand of the Master Saint-Germain at work, again reborn at a strategic time and place in order to gently redirect the wayward education of mankind, in preparation for our emergence into the new age.

Neo-Platonism states that Unity is the Reality; Randomness and Diversification are Illusion. We must seek the Unity, the oneness behind all apparent chaos. Neo-Platonism studies the Universal Principles, and accepts all gods by integrating them into the one God, accepts and unites all men and women as one Humanity. The great Neo-Platonist Truth is that all forms of life are one entity called Life; this is the underlying truth of universal brotherhood—not just for mankind, but for all that is alive in nature.

Neo-Platonism teaches understanding, but not the acceptance of inferior things or thoughts, because perfection is the Truth and anything less is Illusion. Understanding brings unlimited appreciation, and we are advised to practice moderation in all things, so that we may fully appreciate and enjoy the possessions and experiences of life, for excess kills the appetite and smothers enjoyment. We are told to avoid sectarianism, because sects are confined within the walls of Dogma, and dogmatism is the crippler of ideas, originality and creativity.

Neo-Platonism tells us to seek the Good in all people, situations and things—even when what is good may not be pleasant. (It is good, for example to be uncomfortable when we disobey a Universal Law; it is good to be fairly punished when we have hurt others, to be ill when the laws of health have been ignored. For these are warnings that will set us back on an enlightened path.)

And Neo-Platonism tells us that once we have achieved understanding of the primary outlook, and can apply its principles to our own lives, then the student must become the teacher for others. This is one reason why Neo-Platonism is especially practical in today's world.

The Greek intellectuals of his day said that Proclus was a favorite of the gods, that Minerva had raised him since birth and had protected him throughout his life. Proclus himself narrates that when he was very young, Minerva appeared to him and advised him to study philosophy. While he was still a child, he contracted a wasting illness that no doctor could diagnose. His family was gathered at what they thought would be his deathbed, when a young man appeared in the room, rays of brilliant light emanating from his head. The youth approached the bed, placed his finger on Proclus' forehead and spoke only one word: "Proclus." The youth disappeared and the child was instantly cured. Indeed, he was favored by the gods—all of them, gathered into one God.

Proclus continued his studies, following where his mind's inclinations took him. His intellectual capabilities seemed to be unlimited; he himself knew he was destined to be Plato's successor.

In Egypt, he studied under a famous teacher of the time, then entered the school of the hierophants, where he received instruction in the mysteries of the esoteric religion. In Alexandria, he studied under the Greek philosophers, learned mathematics from Hero, a man of deep spiritual values, versed in the mystery of numbers. He studied Aristotelianism under Olympiadorus, a master so impressed with Proclus' abilities that he attempted to match the young man up with his daughter—herself a promising student of philosophy, even in those male-dominated times. But Proclus, then only 20, was interested only in his studies.

He went to Athens, the birthplace and still the world capital of philosophy. There he met Syrianus, a teacher considered the wisest of all men in those days. Syrianus was an expert on the doctrines of Orpheus, Pythagoras and Plato. He took up his studies with the aged Plutarch, who, though he no longer took students, made an exception in this case, and who grew so impressed with Proclus that he took him under his own roof where Proclus stayed until Plutarch's death two years later. Plutarch left instructions to Syrianus, naming him his successor in Proclus' education.

Syrianus taught the young man the Lesser Mysteries, and then initiated him into the Sacred Discipline of Plato. Proclus, through the orderly progression of his own analytical mind, became a recognized leader among the Platonists by the age of 28. By then, he had written quite a few treatises, among them a wise commentary on Plato's Timaeus, a discussion of the forms of good, reality and illusion. He was well on his way to becoming Plato's successor.

Proclus never ate meat, but advised others to eat it occasionally for physical strength. Instead of celebrating the full moon with revelry, as was the Dionysian custom of the day, he celebrated with abstinence and fasting. He advised light foods to philosophy students, since heavy food slows the digestion and interferes with the mental clarity needed to establish Mystical contact with the divinities.

Proclus succeeded Syrianus as Director of the Platonism school in Athens in the year 450, and from that time on dedicated himself wholly to studying and teaching Platonic Mysticism.

The Christians, in the meantime, were quickly undermining the popularity and acceptance of the Greek Mysteries, and Proclus was a prime target for them. Ultimately, their hatred of him forced him to seek refuge in Asia Minor. Merinus, a disciple of Proclus, describes the Christians' actions as "an attack by vultures." In his exile, Proclus studied Law and the mysteries of Oriental philosophy. After a year of such mental enrichment, it had become safe to return to Athens, where he remained for the rest of his life. It was a long and fruitful life; he lived to be 75, a venerable age for any period in history, today included. During his life, he was tolerant of all religions, joining the rites and celebrations of any of them at his pleasure, believing that all religions honored the same higher powers, whatever their names. He enjoyed a wide circle of close friends, bound together in the Pythagoric Brotherhood. After his death in Athens in 485, he was buried in what is now Turkey, in Asia Minor, next to his teacher Syrianus. The epitaph on his tomb was written by himself, and reads: "I, Proclus, having paid my debt to nature, choose to remain in the dust of Lycia. The great Syrianus molded my youth and left me as his successor in the Truth; a common tomb is shared by our bodies, and in the etheric planes is a common place for both our souls."

After this time, the Platonic School of Mysticism ceased to be as a separate entity, and its beliefs were incorporated in the growing body of Christian Metaphysics.

Robert the Monk

*T*here were two monks named Robertus, and because of the sketchy biographical data available from the Middle Ages it is impossible to state with any certainty which of them was the incarnation of Saint-Germain. Both were monks, and both of them were historians, who attempted to document as much as possible human progress through the dark ages. Therefore, I submit a brief description of both of them for your consideration.

The earlier of these was Robert de Torigny, born in 1110. He was a prior or curate at Bee, and later Abbot at Mont Saint-Michel. He wrote historical chronicles covering a period from A.D. 385 through his own lifetime. His writings proved most valuable in their coverage of the Norman-Saxon era, providing historical perspective from both the Anglo and French sides, and going back as early as the Roman occupation of his island, and the Norman invasions.

The second Robert was Robertus de Auxerre, who lived between 1156 and 1211. He was a monk of the monastery at Saint Marien.

Once his historical proclivities were known, the Abbot of his monastery asked him to undertake a monumental task writing a universal history of the world, from creation to his own time. It is not known how much of the project was completed, for he concentrated on divergent periods as individual projects, and other members of the order took up his writings upon his death. During his lifetime, he was known as an outstanding authority on the period between 1181 and 1211—a brief period, historically speaking, but little would be known of it today if it had not been for his work. Many of his original manuscripts are still kept at Auxerre.

Both men followed Saint-Germain's path—maintaining the continuity of human history. But history, ironically, does not tell us enough to allow us to determine which was The Master and which was a far-seeing man of his time.

Roger Bacon

The man who was to become known as "Doctor Mirabilis" was born in 1294, at a time when the Inquisition had been active for 70 years, and he was destined to be a counterbalance for that fanatical institution. His birthplace was Somerset, England, a place where the arms of the Inquisition had never reached. (Had he been born in Spain,

Roger Bacon, the Medical Monk

he might never have seen adulthood, considering his ideas and his outspokenness.)

He was a staunch defender of the esoteric teaching which he (as Proclus) had re-established in the religious traditions. The Inquisition's sole purpose was to maintain the bureaucratic and dogmatic side of the Church in a status quo, by the simple expedient of threatening, torturing and burning at the stake all those who showed signs of "heresy." And one of the most outrageous heresies, to the Church, was the study of any sciences proscribed by the Church or the Bible, most of which were lumped together under the label of "witchcraft." In fact, many of these studies were in the spirit of Jesus—a search for knowledge which was the gift of the Holy Spirit!

He was born the son of a rich farmer who hoped that the son would succeed him in managing the fields, but who found it difficult to make this precocious youngster do anything other than read and ask questions. In desperation, he took the boy to the local priest who was happy to take young Roger in.

However, conflict developed between the father, priest and son as to the direction of his studies, and Roger finally left home to seek refuge at a Franciscan monastery where he could continue his studies undisturbed. Some time later, the Franciscans sent him to Oxford to complete his education, and later to Paris.

Over the years, he had acquired a powerful interest in the occult sciences and he acquired a wealth of knowledge in what is today called "White Magic." Saint-Germain's influence was strongly at work.

Bacon soon became known as the "Father of Occultism." Together with Albert the Magnanimous, Bishop of Ratisbonne, alchemist, scientist and student of white magic and his tutor, Thomas Aquinas, metaphysician, mathematician, logician and mage, he practiced alchemy and the experimental sciences—those mysteries in which Moses and the Egyptians were adepts.

More publicly, Bacon became known for his writings in chemistry, mathematics, astronomy, biology, medicine, metaphysics and engineering. He predicted the development of ships with neither sails nor oars, horseless carriages and flying machines well before Leonardo. In the medical field, he earned the name "Doctor Mirabilis" for his work entitled De Mirabilis Potestate Artis et Natura (Concerning the Marvelous Powers of Art and Nature).

Bacon discovered the usefulness of convex lenses for telescopes and for vision correction. His name is also connected with the discovery and formulation of gunpowder in the western world. His experiments in chemistry naturally led him to the search for the "Philosopher's Stone," the purification of gold and the quest for an Elixir of Life. His researches into the properties of herbs and his knowledge of pharmacology led him to develop a formula that he was later to mention—as Saint-Germain—as the secret of his longevity.

Roger Bacon fought for freedom of thought in an era of ignorance and resistance to new ideas, and naturally he made many enemies—to the extent that he was persecuted and ultimately cast out of his Order by his fellow Franciscans. He attempted to find refuge in Paris, the site of his earlier studies, but there, too, he found a restrictive and stultifying regime. In his time, his fiery ego managed to alienate many of his former associates, including his brothers, both Franciscan and Dominican, as well as Bishop Albert the Magnanimous and Thomas Aquinas (whom he referred to as "ignorant and illiterate" in matters of philosophy and metaphysics).

Ultimately he appealed to Pope Clement IV, who expressed a desire to have copies of his writings. Though burdened by financial problems, he was able to complete his Opus Majus, Opus Minus and

Opus Tertium Written in Latin, as were all studious works at the time, these found favor with the Pope, which made it possible for Bacon to return to Oxford to further his scientific studies. There, he wrote a lengthy treatise which probed the inconsistencies, contradictions and errors between Philosophy and Theology. This so displeased England's ecclesiastical authorities that he was jailed and all his books burned.

Despite the restrictive times he lived in, Roger Bacon's intellectual energy made itself known. He was the first to declare that observation and experimentation were essential to the accumulation of scientific knowledge, and that all phenomena, whether physical or psychical, cannot be studied effectively without experimentation.

Some stories about Roger Bacon demonstrate his flair for the dramatic in making his points—and perhaps also demonstrate the effectiveness of his communion with the Astral Plane.

It is said that once when the King of England was visiting the estate of a nobleman in Oxfordshire, he expressed an interest in meeting the famous monk. The master of the castle sent a messenger to find him at Oxford. Bacon agreed to come and told the messenger, "You go on ahead to announce my arrival—although I'd better warn you that I shall arrive before you." The messenger laughed and wagered an undisclosed sum that Bacon could not possibly beat him to the castle, whereupon he left for that destination immediately.

Bacon arrived at the castle and was welcomed by the king, who asked for a demonstration of his legendary abilities. He accepted, saying, "I will please several of your senses, Your Majesty." He produced a wand and made several flourishes in the air. Suddenly, the room was filled with beautiful music. He gestured again and dancers appeared, performing a ballet to the music. Another wave of the wand and the air was filled with perfume. The dancers disappeared, and in their place was a banquet table filled with delicious foods. It was no illusion, for monarch and quests ate heartily. The king was highly impressed, and said that he would grant Bacon a favor. Roger replied that his only wish was to be in the king's good graces. The king assured him of his and his court's affection, and insisted on giving him a precious gem.

At that point, Bacon commented, "There seems to be someone missing—the messenger Your Highness sent to fetch me." All present searched for the man, and one guest finally saw him approaching. The messenger appeared, and was so confused and frustrated at finding Bacon there well ahead of him that he shouted angrily at the monk. To calm him, Bacon said, "I have a special manifestation for you, my friend—look." So saying, he parted one of the heavy draperies to reveal one of the kitchen maids, ladle in hand, and quite startled at being discovered. "I am sure," he added, "that this lovable child would be very helpful in your kitchen. But, since I don't know your financial situation, I'll be happy to pay for her trip to your house." With those words, the girl disappeared.

Such flamboyance, in varying degrees, was typical of the entertainment provided by the bards and actors of the middle ages— though not of monks. Bacon's performance was beyond the abilities of ordinary entertainers, since he had the advantage of his great knowledge, and the collaboration of the elementals of the Astral or Psychic Plane. (Elementals are not to be trifled with by anyone but the most adept; they are difficult to dislodge from their own plane, and it is even more difficult to return them there. Haunted houses, appearances of ghosts, even visits from the devil can be most often ascribed to elementals who are seeking to widen the gateway to our physical plane.)

Such an appearance is mentioned in another tale told about Roger Bacon. An elemental disguised as the devil appeared to a man who was deeply in debt, offering him great sums of money as long as the man promised to give the "devil" his soul after paying all his debts. The man accepted and, thinking himself clever, paid his debts as slowly as possible, being in no hurry to conclude the contract. But finally, when he couldn't make his creditors wait any longer, he was forced to pay all. At that point, he began to contemplate suicide. Bacon, seeing the man's despair, asked him the reason for it.

The man told him the facts, and the monk told him: "Go to your place of appointment with the devil, but refuse his demands. When he continues to claim his due, demand that an arbitrator judge the matter—and be sure to insist that your judge be the first person who happens by."

The man did as he was told, demanding that the first passerby be his judge, and the devil grudgingly agreed. After a brief wait, Friar Bacon appeared, and the debtor stopped him and explained the situation. The devil added, "The facts are clear. He agreed that, once all his debts were paid, he would pay me with his soul. He's finished paying, and his time is up."

The monk answered, "The facts are indeed clear—if it is indeed true that he has paid all his debts."

"Ask him yourself," the devil said. And the man tremblingly agreed that he owed no one.

"But," Bacon continued, "is it not true that you still owe the devil his due, and that you both consider this a legitimate debt?" The man admitted that he had not paid the devil a thing. "In that case," said Bacon, "give him nothing, and you are free."

To the devil, he said, "The agreement was that he must give you his soul once he was free of debt. Since his soul is itself a debt you cannot collect it without violating the agreement. Now go—disappear in the name of the Holy Cross."

Outlogicked, the "devil" disappeared in a burst of flame.

Spiritualists have long since learned the folly of involving elementals in matters of the Earthly Plane. And tales such as this point out the dangers.

Roger Bacon continued his studies and his teachings. He was jailed for various "offenses" to the Church in 1278 and was not released for fourteen years. He continued teaching the Truth of all sciences, including Metaphysics until his death, only two years later, in 1294.

Christian Rosenkreutz

*C*hristian Rosenkreutz, the founder of the Rosicrucians, was born in Germany in 1378 and died in 1484. He was the orphaned son of noble parents, and was raised in the religious life, educated in a monastery, where he learned to write in both Latin and Greek, as did most learned men of his time.

The Christian religion at the time was poorly understood and badly taught. The inquisition was in force, and just coming into its greatest influence in Spain, where Torquemada was soon to emerge as its leader. It was a time when Saint-Germain's efforts to steer mankind into Christ's path were sorely needed, and they found expression in his incarnation as Rosenkreutz.

When he was 17, Rosenkreutz, accompanied by one of the monks, left the monastery that had been his home and traveled to Damascus, Jerusalem, the Arab countries, Egypt, Morocco and Spain. To Rosenkreutz' sorrow, his companion died in Cyprus, and the young man resolved to continue his travels alone. In Damascus, he heard of a secret society of Theosophists in the city of Damcar and was anxious to meet them. He arrived there on his 18th birthday, and was most graciously received by the members of the circle—in fact, they told him that they had been waiting for his arrival for quite a while, though there was no way of their knowing he was on his way. He was further mystified by the fact that the Brothers were able to recount to him certain events of his lifetime that they could not have known by other than mystical means. It was obvious that they had much to teach him about the occult arts, and he decided to stay with them.

He was initiated into the mysteries and learned Arabic well enough to translate a book of their encyclopedia into Latin. After three years of study with the Theosophists, he was judged ready to expand his educational horizons. He left Damcar for Egypt and then on to Fez, where he found other Masters who taught him how to invoke the elemental spirits. After two years of study in Fez, he moved on to Spain, where he found what he had learned was in conflict with the teachings of the "learned" men of that country. He tried to point out the inconsistencies, but he was received with laughter and told that the erudites of Spain had received their tutelage in the "Black Arts" at the University of Salamanca—from none other than Satan himself. He was filled with indignation at this corruption of the occult arts, and left Spain for other countries—but found much the same treatment wherever he went. He finally returned to his own country, where he remained a recluse, devoting his time to studies and his writing.

After five years of this hermit's life, he decided that someone such as he, who had achieved the transmutation of metals and developed the elixir of life, was destined for a nobler purpose in life than to close himself off from the world. His purpose was to help his fellows, not abandon them.

Slowly, he began building a circle of confidantes and devotees who were to become the nucleus of the future Rosicrucian society. He and four brothers in his group developed a secret language of magic and produced a dictionary of Occult wisdom, which they entitled: All That

Man Can Wish For, Ask For and Hope For. He translated the works and wisdom of Solomon, Moses and Enoch into Latin. He organized the first Rosicrucian Society, calling it "The House of the Holy Spirit." And when the order had reached eight Brothers in number, he decided it was time to spread the Truth, through chapters in other countries throughout the world. They agreed to maintain the society in complete secrecy for one hundred years.

And the Order grew slowly but steadily under the veil of secrecy. Christian Rosenkreutz lived to the age of 106, and was buried in one of the secret houses of the Order. It wasn't until the third generation of successors to the original members that his tomb was discovered in a hidden crypt. It was inscribed with the magical characters of the order, and the body was in a state of perfect preservation. (It is said that the cells in the bodies of the truly Enlightened are literally filled with cleansing light, and cannot deteriorate.) Buried with him were many important documents which cleared up many disagreements between the various chapters of the order. Some chapters had even begun to doubt Rosenkreutz' existence as anything more, than a symbol, since each chapter managed to find some evidence that it was the original House. One document ordered that the teachings and purposes of the Society be spread publicly to all sincere and educated persons who expressed interest.

In 1614, the philosophers, alchemists and scientists of Cassel, Germany, were surprised by the publication of a pamphlet entitled Fama Fraternitates: Or Fraternal Opinions of the Meritorious Order of the Rose Cross, directed to the intelligentsia in general, as well as to the heads of governments in Europe. It was a message from a group of anonymous adepts who were deeply disturbed by the human condition and who yearned for a human renaissance. It proposed that all sincere men unite to establish a scientific synthesis that would find the ideal system for the study and growth of the occult arts. It called for an end to discord and conflict among intellectuals and for the dissolution of authorities who stifled man with their antiquated theories. And it stressed the fact that, just as religion had undergone a Reformation, so science was much in need of the same process, to weed out the dogma and deadwood that had held back scientific progress for so long. It proposed that such a process be directed by a Brotherhood of the Enlightened, who had been initiated in the mysteries of the Orient by a high-ranking member of the Hierarchy of Adepts, and who would be capable of leading this era to a state of Perfection. There were seven editions of this pamphlet in three years, and it captured the attention of many of the West's leading thinkers. Such men as Jakob Bohme, Goethe and Wagner were influenced by these ideas, moved by the spirit that rejected the confines of orthodox religion, dogmas and mental slavery to seek freedom for the children of God in a new form.

The Brothers of the Rosicrucian Order agreed that the spirit of the founder enjoyed continued physical existence through the process of borrowed bodies, taking on a new form for every change in endeavor. Which, of course, agrees with Master Saint-Germain's communications regarding his appearance in more than forty such "borrowed" bodies.

Sir Francis Bacon

Sir Francis Bacon lived from 1561 to 1628. History tells us that he was the son of Sir Nicholas Bacon and Lady Anne Cooke—but Court gossip has it that he might possibly have been the son of Queen Elizabeth I and Sir Robert Dudley, Count of Leicester and a favorite among favorites at Court. It is known that Elizabeth and Dudley planned a secret marriage in 1560, but that affairs of state interfered; still, there were numerous clandestine meetings. A few months after the last of these meetings, a new fashion in dress dominated the court: A woodhard, pointed waistline that went from the bodice down, surrounded by voluminous "polissons" at each side and over the hips.

Sir Francis Bacon

It was flattering to few, but was ideal for disguising an unwanted pregnancy.

Valuing her right to reign uninfluenced, she had apparently abandoned her plans for marriage, and continued to be known as the "Virgin Queen." As for the child, it would have had to have been adopted by someone of rank in the Court. Sir Nicholas would have been ideal.

Whoever his parents were, young Francis proved to be a highly intelligent child. He entered Trinity College at the age of twelve and Cambridge three years later. He showed a marked inclination toward philosophy, politics and diplomacy—and, even at 16, demonstrated an equally obvious aversion to the philosophy of Aristotle, which he found sterile and totally devoid of ideas which could benefit mankind in any practical fashion.

When he had finished his University studies, the Bacons sent him to Paris, under the tutelage of the English Ambassador, to further his studies in politics and diplomacy. It was there that he became interested in the experimental sciences. During this time, he brought to light the fact that the first (Greek) scientists were interested only in verbal, intellectual discussion, formulating theories through "pure reason" derived from the most casual observation. Modern science, he said, should concern itself with discovering nature's secrets through observation and repeated experimentation, the blending of theory and practice. It was the same championship of the modern Scientific Method, the same thinking that characterized all of Saint-Germain's incarnations.

He began writing a major work at this time, Instauratio Magno de Dignitarius Scientarum (The Great Renewal of the Worth of the Sciences), a book destined to create a wave of new thought among the scientists of the 16th and 17th centuries.

Fate, in the form of his father's death, brought him back to London. As the second son of the family, his share of the inheritance was a meager one, and he was forced to consider more "practical" means of earning a living; this led him to begin his studies in Law.

After his father's death, Francis was taken under the protective wing of Lord Burghley, his uncle on his mother's side. However that protection proved intensely humiliating and stultifying: Burghley seemed to feel that his tutelage of the young man should be expressed as domination and repression. All of young Bacon's attempts to gain advancement at Court were in vain. (It may have been that the Queen did not wish a reminder of her past so near at hand.)

Finally, however, Burghley did manage to obtain a seat in Parliament for him, hoping that this would satisfy him. But Bacon was no meek instrument; one of his first acts was to stand against a Royal Petition. This did not endear him to the Queen or his uncle, and marked the end of any special favors granted him.

Nonetheless, it was almost impossible to hold him back; his public reputation for his scientific and literary works continued to grow, even at times of the strongest opposition. In 1605, he published the first section of his Instauratio Magno under the title Divine and Human Knowledge, and it won immediate attention from the great minds of England.

With Sir Francis Bacon, the modem age of Philosophy was born. He became a Rosicrucian and was raised to the level of Imperator in the Society. He published an answer to Aristotle's Organum, entitled Novum Organum. He tried to free the intellectuals of his time from the restrictions of Aristotelian theology and philosophy, and (as in his previous incarnations) re-established the values of Neo-Platonism.

Upon Queen Elizabeth's death in 1603, James I ascended to the throne. The new monarch held no animosity for Bacon, and it was not long before his skills and abilities were rewarded with position. He was first named Procurer, then Fiscal to the Crown, and Lord Protector of the Royal Seal (a position once held by Thomas à Becket) and then Royal Counselor, all in the space of 11 years. He was also given the title of Lord Verulam and, three years later, (most appropriately) Viscount St.-Albans.

All great men have enemies—usually lesser people who think that by opposing the great they can somehow measure up to their stature. And Bacon's rapid advancement produced considerable envy and ill feelings. He was verbally attacked. Lies and rumors were circulated. Eventually some of these found the ears of highly-placed people and he was jailed in the Tower of London. Bacon was a staunch defender of the King's policies, but Elizabeth's many supporters in the court prevailed for a while. Ultimately, James had him released and reinstated to his former position; but Bacon had seen enough of court politics, and retired to private life where he continued to speak out against social conditions and worked on his Instauratio Magno until his death in 1626.

It was said that Francis Bacon was buried in the Church of Saint Michael of Verulam at the Cathedral of St. Albans, however, there is no body in the tomb, and recent evidence indicates that there never was.

This seems like a good time to talk about the power of a name. From the most primitive times to the present day, people have known instinctively that a person's name is a dominating influence. Native Americans, Africans and many other peoples have long believed that a person should be known publicly by one name, but that one's true name should only be known to one's most trusted intimates. The theme is common throughout world mythology and religion, even extending to the summoning power one has over a demon (elemental) by being able to pronounce his true name.

There is a basis for this, and it lies in the spectrum of Vibration. The name a mother chooses for her child is chosen as an instinctive response to the vibrations of the Ego she carries within her. Should a name be chosen that the mother feels is wrong for the child, we will see frustration in that child's development and future life, an inability to live up to his or her fullest potential. (Even the most successful people are often frustrated, knowing they can do more, but somehow fall short of their own expectations.) And, conversely, many times we will see frustration turn to success when a person changes his name to one more suitable.

Now, consider Sir Francis Bacon. Having been given the same surname twice, he found himself trapped in this penultimate incarnation, forced to repeat much of the work he had accomplished as Roger Bacon. He was further drawn backwards to even earlier names: to Albans, to Verulam (Verulamium, St. Albans' birthplace).

Fortunately, Bacon's—Saint-Germain's—was a powerful ego, able to draw on past accomplishments and subconscious knowledge, and he was able to accomplish much of what he set out to do.

Still, it makes one wonder.

What if he actually was the child of Elizabeth I? What If he had become the successor to the British throne? What marvels of social and scientific progress might have been brought to the world by the first metaphysician-King of this powerful empire?

Ascended Master Saint-Germain

Saint-Germain, Ascended Master

*A*s I mentioned earlier, the Master Saint-Germain has recently undergone another stage in his evolution. After having given mankind the amazing gift known as the Transmuting Violet Flame, which frees men from "karma," from "purgatory," from the punishments men have inflicted on themselves, frees them from all misdirected energy and from all "human creations" by the Law of the Circle, he has been given his reward by the Supreme Presence—the title of God of Freedom.

Master Saint-Germain said in a previous communiqué: "My name disappeared with my past." Today, he says: "I AM the sun of freedom, and it is my great privilege to spread the cause of freedom across the planet."

The enlightened esoteric writer David Anrias, in his book Adepts of the Five Elements, explains much about what he calls "the chaos of our times." He describes how the misdirection of our search for the polar self, the duality that lies within us, result in unfortunate side-effects of the new age's search for self-awareness. Instead of examining the inner self, some turn to that outward expression of the duality of self. But we are cleansing ourselves of thousands of years of accumulated destructive energy, thanks to the efforts of such masters as Saint-Germain, and soon we shall be able to visualize Truth more clearly.

The growing drug problem, too, Anrias sees as a misdirected search for Truth. Altered states of perception and awareness, feelings of intense pleasure, brought on through artificial means, are easily mistaken by the innocent and uninitiated for visions of Truth and

Ascended Master Saint-Germain

Beauty. And here, again, we must seek that Truth within ourselves, within the I AM Presence of God that is in every one of us. Drugs do not tear aside the veils of perception, but further obscure our vision. We should be able to live in eternal youth and beauty, eternal happiness, without problems, illness or wrongdoing, but we have ignored Spiritual Truth; we are stationary because we refuse to see what lies beyond the physical plane.

The Planetary Directors, Saint-Germain and the other Ascended Masters and the Cosmic and Angelic Hosts will have prepared to pour in vain, all the Light we need to uplift our planet—unless we ourselves open the door for that light to enter. That invitation must come from us, and if it does not, even God will not intervene, because He will not break his own Law of Free Will.

This book has been written in the hope of revealing all the efforts which the Master Saint-Germain has made to bring us gradually to the acme of our Ascension as individuals, as a species, as an expression of Life.

We must do all in our power to cleanse ourselves and the emanations from our planet. Repeating the following formula three times a day for five minutes each time will help:

In the name of the Beloved I AM Presence, I invoke the freeing Violet Flame to surround and illuminate all the energy points of our planet, and all its inhabitants, incarnate and disincarnate, until all becomes pure and radiant. I thank you, Father, for I know you have heard me.

As you do so, visualize the Violet Flame surrounding your own body; let it expand to illuminate your house, your neighborhood, city, country, and the entire planet. May the radiance of the Flame enfold us all!

Bibliography

Gentleman's Magazine, London, 1745.

Music Chronicle, London. 1746.

Letters from Horace Walpole, Archives, Holland, 1760.

Weekly Journal, London, 1760.

Chateau de Chambord, National Archives, Blois, 1760.

Affaires Etrangères, Paris, 11760.

"Memoires Anecdotiques de Louis XV," London Chronicle, June 3, 1760.

Graf Saint-Germain, Oettinger, 1840.

Remarkable Adventures and Unrevealed Mysteries, L. Wrexall, London, R. Bentley, 1863.

Voltaire's Complete Works, Firmin Didot, Paris, 1877.

Memoires of Mme. de Hausset, Firmin Didot, Paris, 1877.

Historical Mysteries, Andrew Lang, 1904.

Secret Societies, Una Birch, London, 1911.

Memoires of Mme. de Genlis, Pompadour's Handmaid, Paris, 1928.

La Marquise de Pompadour, Paris, 1938.

Le Comte de Saint-Germain, Paris, 1938.

Memoires Authentiques de Cagliostro.

Correspondence de Grim et Voltaire.

Foreign Affairs, Carlos de Villermont and Le Comte de Cobenzle, London.

A Stranger Passed, Catherine Christian, 1960.

Roger Bacon, Marvelous Doctor, Liam Brophy, 1963.

The Enigmatic Count Saint-Germain, Pierre Ceria and Francois Ethuin, 1972.

L'Incostanza Delusa, recording, Count Saint-Germain, available from: Philosophical Research Society, 3910 Los Feliz Park Boulevard, Los Angeles, CA.

Biography of Conny Méndez

1898-1979

Early Life - Before Metaphysics

*C*onny Méndez was nothing if not courageous. She was born Juana María de la Concepción Méndez Guzmán, but from an early age she happily adopted the nickname "Conny" given to her by the nuns at the Sacred Heart Convent School in New York. Once back in her native Venezuela, and despite a repressive culture, she followed her artistic dreams and later in life had a spiritual awakening that would give birth to a movement.

Influenced by her years abroad, she was something of a trailblazer in her own country. The first divorce on record in Venezuela was hers, and she was the first woman to wear a bathing suit and smoke cigarettes in public—quite unheard of at the time.

Conny used to say that she was born too early and would have loved to have been able to express her free spirit as a "hippie" in the 1960s. It's easy to understand why. Coming from the rigid upper class of Caracas society at the turn of the century, she attended strict Catholic boarding schools; where girls had to bathe wearing big canvas ponchos to avoid looking at their "shameful" bodies.

She humorously recounted her life's story in a memoir she titled *Las memorias de una loca* Barquisimeto, Venezuela 1955 (Memoirs of a Madwoman) currently available in the anthology, *La chispa de Conny Méndez. Humor y memorias*, Caracas, Venezuela 2007 (The wit of Conny Méndez. Humor and Memoirs).

Multitalented "toera" (jack-of-all-trades)

*I*n spite of the lack of options available for women in the Venezuela of the early 20th century, Conny made a name for herself as a caricaturist, composer, lyricist, humorist, actress, and later in life, an author of popular books on what she termed, "Christian Metaphysics" based on the teachings of Unity, Emmet Fox, the Ascended Masters, and other New Thought leaders of the 20th century. She dedicated the rest of her life to living, studying, and teaching these principles, and wrote prolifically in her "palabras de a centavo" (penny words) which were, as she described, "the simplest words even a 10-year-old could understand." The books and periodicals she wrote on metaphysics were distributed throughout Latin America and the Spanish-speaking world.

Composer

*A*t the age of five, Conny composed a "nocturne" on the family piano. There would be more than 50 other compositions; among these, a heart-wrenching love song, called *Déjame* (Leave me). But, her best-known musical body of work is a celebration of the Venezuela she knew and loved; songs that instilled a sense of national pride in her fellow countrymen. *Venezuela habla cantando*, (Venezuela speaks in song), *Yo soy venezolana*, (I am Venezuelan) are two of the most well-known.

She toured Spain in the early 1950s as a kind of Venezuelan cultural ambassador, wearing traditional dress, playing guitar, and singing her own folkloric compositions. These songs remain part of a national musical legacy and are still recorded and sung by Venezuelan singers and musicians all over the world.

Multicultural Translator

Conny lived for a time in the United States and France, and spoke perfect English and French with no trace of an accent. She was a prolific translator as well. Several of her metaphysical books were translated from the original English-language versions by one of her favorite authors, Godfrè Ray King. Her trilingual fluency allowed her to navigate seamlessly among multiple cultures.

Personal life

Conny married three times. She was divorced twice and was widowed by her third husband, a Spanish movie director in Mexico. She had two children. A daughter, Julieta (1920-2018), with her first husband, and a son, Donald (1931-), with her second husband. Three of her seven grandchildren are currently involved in perpetuating the legacy of their remarkable grandmother.

Introduction to Metaphysics

Conny was introduced to metaphysics on a voyage from New York to Caracas, in 1945, before the end of WWII. A sister ship, in nearby waters, had fallen victim to an enemy mine, and when the news reached her ship, Conny, like most passengers, was terrified. One night, she observed the wife of renowned botanist, Henry Pittier, laughing and singing with some passengers and crew. Conny insisted that this woman explain how she could be so gleeful in the face of such imminent danger. Mrs. Pittier credited Dr. Emmet Fox's teachings and graciously shared her copy of his book *Find and Use Your Inner Power,* which Conny subsequently devoured. The ship arrived safely, and Conny was forever changed. From then on, Dr. Fox became one of Conny's favorite teachers, and so began her passion for metaphysics.

For more information on Conny Méndez, please visit:

Web: www.connymendez.com
YouTube: www.youtube.com/ConnyMendezMetafisica
Facebook: www.facebook.com/ConnyMendezMetafisica
Twitter: @connymendez
Instagram: @connymendez

Metaphysical Collection

Power Through Metaphysics in other languages:

Spanish Vol. I
ISBN 9789806329478

Spanish Vol. II
ISBN 9789806114098

Spanish Vol. III
ISBN 9789803690991

Italian
ISBN 9788863240542

French
ISBN 9789963241372

Japanese, part I
ISBN 9784864714600

Japanese, part II
ISBN 9784864714617

Metaphysical Collection
in Spanish

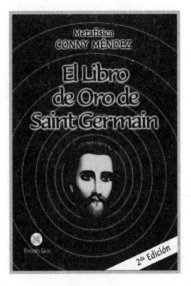

2da
Edición

El Libro de Oro
de la Hermandad Saint Germain

Esta es la Sagrada Enseñanza que el Maestro Ascendido Saint Germain ha dispuesto para esta, Su Era de Oro, y que forma el Tercer Ciclo de Enseñanza de la Hermandad Saint Germain, después de lo cual el discípulo queda en conocimiento pleno de su Presencia «**Yo Soy**».

El Libro de Oro de Saint Germain - Traducción y adaptación original de Conny Méndez del libro en inglés: *The "I Am" discourses* por el Ascendido Maestro Saint Germain. El título en español *El Libro de Oro de Saint Germain* es original de Conny Méndez ©.

Formato 12 x 17 cmts. 320 pgs.
ISBN: 978-980-6114-85-2

2da
Edición

Misterios Develados

*E*sta serie de libros está dedicada con el más profundo Amor Eterno y Gratitud a nuestro amado Maestro Saint Germain, la Gran Hermandad Blanca, la Hermandad del Royal Teton, la Hermandad del Monte Shasta, y a aquellos Maestros Ascendidos cuya ayuda amorosa ha sido directa e ilimitada.

El propósito de poner este libro en manos del público es para comunicarle al individuo el valor y la fuerza que ha de sostenerlo a través de este período de transición en que vivimos.

Misterios Develados - Traducción y adaptación: Conny Méndez. Título original en inglés: *Unveiled Mysteries* por Godfré Ray King.

Formato 12 x 17 cmts. 272 páginas.
ISBN: 978-980-6114-10-4

2da Edición

La Mágica Presencia

*E*sta serie de libros está dedicada con el más profundo amor y eterna gratitud a nuestros amados Maestros Ascendidos, Saint Germain, Jesús, Nada, El Gran Divino Director, nuestro Amado Mensajero Ascendido, Guy W. Ballard, la Gran Hermandad Blanca, la Hermandad del Royal Tetón, la Hermandad del monte Shasta, los Grandes Maestros Ascendidos de Venus, los Grandes Seres Cósmicos, la Gran Hueste Angélica, La Gran Luz Cósmica; y todos aquellos otros Maestros Ascendidos, cuya ayuda amorosa ha sido directa y sin límites.

La Mágica Presencia - Continuación de *Misterios Develados*. Traducción y adaptación: Conny Méndez. Título original en inglés: *The Magic Presence* por Godfré Ray King.

Formato 13,3 x 20,5 cmts. 288 pgs.
ISBN: 978-980-6114-15-9

2ta Edición

El Nuevo Pensamiento

*E*sta publicación es una recopilación de las únicas nueve revistas del mismo nombre cuya directora y autora fue Conny Méndez, que circularon desde 1970 hasta 1972. Es una lectura muy interesante para los estudiantes de Metafísica porque en ella se encuentran temas sumamente variados. Todo el empeño de lo que divulga el Nuevo Pensamiento Metafísico es acelerar lo más posible la venida de esa Edad de Oro y que todos los humanos puedan participar rápidamente de este tesoro.

Formato 13,3 x 21,0 cmts. 304 pgs.
ISBN: 978-980-6114-14-2

2da
Edición

La Voz Del «Yo Soy»

U na vez que Conny Méndez terminó de publicar la revista *El Nuevo Pensamiento*, entre 1970 y 1972, continuó con la dirección y edición de pequeños folletos que denominó *La Voz del «Yo Soy»*. Recopiló varios artículos relacionados con el aprendizaje y aportó otros escritos de su autoría. Los nombres de los instructores de Metafísica que Conny formó para la continuación de la enseñanza están en una lista en el apéndice de la presente edición.

En esta revista, ahora en formato de libro, al igual que en la anterior, se ofrecen diversos temas que el estudiante metafísico supo agradecer y tiene como mérito el haber sido reproducida manualmente por la autora en un pequeño multígrafo casero de marca Gestetner procedente de Inglaterra.

Formato 13,3 x 21,0 cmts. 176 pgs.
ISBN: 978-980-6114-42-6

2da
Edición

Palabras de los Maestros Ascendidos
Volumen I

*U*na vez más Conny Méndez nos obsequia su magistral traducción de los discursos pronunciados por los Maestros Ascendidos, que son todos aquellos grandes seres cósmicos de tal majestad y poder que difícilmente la mente humana puede captar.

El poder que manejan es ilimitado y en este justo momento se encuentran vigilando todas las actividades constructivas del mundo, dispuestos a liberar cualquier poder de sus Rayos de Luz cuando se requiera para dar protección a aquellos que sinceramente buscan y sirven a la Luz.

Cada discurso está poderosamente cargado con la Vida, la Luz y el Amor de cada Maestro Cósmico.

En este primer volumen se ofrecen los primeros 12 discursos de los Maestros Cósmicos Jesús, Saint Germain, Lady Nada, El Gran Director Divino, Sanat Kumara, El Amado Cyclopea, El Guardián Silencioso, La Poderosa Astrea, Lord Maitreya, El Maha Chohan, El Amado Lanto y Lady Leto. Estos discursos fueron dictados a lo largo del año 1937. Se incluye la lámina de la Magna Presencia «Yo Soy», tal como se presenta en el libro original, y las imágenes de los Maestros Jesús y Saint Germain.

Formato 13,3 x 21,0 cmts. 184 pgs.
ISBN: 978-980-12-9823-6

2da
Edición

Palabras de los Maestros Ascendidos
Volumen II

Continuación del libro *Palabras de los Maestros Ascendidos*, Volumen I, aquí se ofrecen los siguientes 15 discursos de los Maestros Cósmicos Chamada, Amado Pelleur, dios Tabor, dios Himalaya, Koot Hoomi, El Morya, Hilarión, Serapis Bey, Gran Tenor Cósmico, Madre María, Reina de Luz, diosa de La Libertad, Amado David Lloyd, Amado Victory. Y para finalizar, la Bendición del Cristo en la Llama Violeta. Estos discursos fueron dictados a lo largo de los años 1937 y 1938

Se incluye la lámina de la Magna Presencia «Yo Soy» e imágenes de los Maestros Koot Hoomi, El Morya, Hilarión y Amado Victory.

Formato 13,3 x 21,0 cmts. 224 pgs.
ISBN: 978-980-12-9824-3

4ta
Edición

La Chispa de Conny Méndez
Humor y Memorias

*L*a Chispa Venezolana de Conny Méndez, originalmente publicado en 1980, contenía sus memorias humorísticas *Las Memorias de una Loca* (Barquisimeto, 1955), su versión de la historia de Venezuela Histori-Comi-Sátira *Del Guayuco al Quepis* (Caracas, 1967) y el álbum de caricaturas *Bisturí* (París, 1931). En siguientes ediciones, se insertó el cuento esotérico *Entre Planos* (Caracas 1958), se incluyó una Cronología que vincula los eventos más importantes en la vida de Conny Méndez con su producción artística, y para finalizar, se agregaron fotografías para ilustrar personas, momentos y rasgos artísticos de la polifacética Conny Méndez.

Formato 15 x 21.5 cmts. 272 pgs.
ISBN: 978-980-6114-43-2

Conny Méndez

*L*a caraqueñísima Conny Méndez, dicho por ella misma, era una toera porque hacía de todo. Fue una venezolana fuera de lo común; es posible que muchos jóvenes no hayan oído nunca el nombre de esta extraordinaria mujer.

Fue bautizada como Juana María de la Concepción, para dejarlo en Conchita. Era hija de Eugenio Méndez y Mendoza, escritor y poeta de finísima calidad, y de Lastenia Guzmán de Méndez y Mendoza.

Conny estuvo adelantada a su época, y allá por el año 1927 cuando las mujeres fumaban a escondidas, ella lo hacía en público y decía que ya se lo agradecerían las caraqueñas algún día, según cuentan sus allegados.

Desde muy joven se dedicó a casi todo y más o menos por orden cronológico fue de la siguiente manera: Autora y Compositora. Su primera composición fue *La niña luna*, que realizó y a manera de ensayo. Posteriormente compuso *La Negrita Marisol, Yo soy venezolana, Venezuela habla cantando y Chucho y Ceferina*, por citar solo cuatro, y esta última es considerada por muchos como ejemplo de música folklórica. Luego vinieron muchísimas otras, algunas de ellas de enorme difusión conocidas por toda Venezuela y como cantautora deleitó a millares de personas interpretando sus propias piezas durante muchísimos años, tanto en el país como en el extranjero.

Como caricaturista y cronista trabajó en la revista *Nosotras* en su columna Aquí entre nos. Conny también fue pintora; comenzó en este campo haciendo paisajes y retratos. Durante 10 años gozó "un puyero" con sus paletas, pinceles y demás yerbas (como se expresaba), y llegó a terminar un sinnúmero de obras cuyo paradero ella desconoció, dado que muchas se las llevaban "prestadas, y la gente, lamentablemente, tiene tan mala memoria", decía.

Como escritora se proyectó principalmente a través de su libro *Memorias de una loca*, publicado en 1955, que hoy se conoce como *La Chispa de Conny Méndez, Humor y Memorias* y que resultó todo un bestseller. Es una recopilación de lo más divertido que le había ocurrido hasta entonces, sus caricaturas, su versión de la historia de Venezuela Histori-Comi-Sátira y un cuento esotérico.

Como si todo esto fuera poco hay que resaltar la dedicación casi total que Conny Méndez le brindó a su gran pasión: la Metafísica. Una vez que se encontraba a bordo de un tanquero que la traía desde Estados Unidos durante la Segunda Guerra Mundial, conoció a la esposa de Henry Pittier. Esta dama inició a Conny en el mundo de la Metafísica. El viaje resultó toda una odisea y, por supuesto, en muchos momentos hizo falta mucha fe en Dios para sobrellevar el peso del tremendo peligro que les acechaba. En esos momentos Conny y la señora Pittier hablaron mucho de Filosofía y de Metafísica. Al llegar a Venezuela –"milagrosamente" como dijo Conny–, se lanzó de lleno a la búsqueda de cualquier material literario que existiera sobre Metafísica. Leyó todo lo que cayó en sus manos y un día, profundamente conocedora de esta filosofía, fundó la Hermandad de Saint Germain que se extendió, primero, por toda Venezuela, y luego por toda Latinoamérica. Y en este campo siguió tan activa que viajó y dictó conferencias, y se comunicó con los miles de amigos que tenía en todas partes.

Su producción más notable la constituyen cuatro pequeños tomos de Metafísica: *Metafísica al alcance de todos*, *Te regalo lo que se te antoje*, *El maravilloso Número 7* y *¿Quién es y quién fue el Conde Saint Germain?*, recopilados en un solo volumen titulado *Metafísica 4 en 1*.

Por todas estas razones no se exagera un ápice al tildar a Conny como una venezolana totalmente fuera de lo común.

Funda en 1946 el movimiento de Metafísica Cristiana en Venezuela, consagrándose de lleno a la enseñanza esotérica a través de sus libros y conferencias. Fue condecorada en tres ocasiones con: Diploma y Botón de Oro Cuatricentenario, 1967; Diploma y Medalla de Buen Ciudadano, 1968; Orden Diego de Losada en 2a. Clase, 1976. Recibió además, en reconocimiento de su labor artística, cultural y humanitaria, numerosos homenajes y galardones, así como diversas placas en reconocimiento de su labor en el campo de la Metafísica Cristiana.

☨

Para más información nos puede visitar:
Web: www.connymendez.com
YouTube: www.youtube.com/ConnyMendezMetafisica
Facebook: www.facebook.com/ConnyMendezMetafisica
Twitter: @connymendez
Instagram: @connymendez

Este libro se terminó de imprimir en
el mes de noviembre de 2020 en Romanyà Valls, S.A.
Capellades (Barcelona).